Lewis H Blair

The Prosperity of the South Dependent Upon the Elevation of the

Negro

Lewis H Blair

The Prosperity of the South Dependent Upon the Elevation of the Negro

ISBN/EAN: 9783337424411

Printed in Europe, USA, Canada, Australia, Japan

Cover: Foto ©Suzi / pixelio.de

More available books at **www.hansebooks.com**

PROSPERITY OF THE SOUTH

DEPENDENT UPON THE

ELEVATION OF THE NEGRO

BY

LEWIS H. BLAIR,

AUTHOR OF

"UNWISE LAWS."

RICHMOND, VA.:
EVERETT WADDEY.
1889.

PREFACE.

In discussing great themes, in contemplating great subjects, it is essential, in order to arrive at a true interpretation or to reach a wise decision, to take into consideration great causes and broad effects.

In the lower realms of animal life we can sever and dissever, and each segment at once begins a new and separate existence entirely independent of its parent form. But when we ascend higher, bisection means destruction, and equally when we approach the grand region of humanity, and its vast concerns, we cannot cut into fragments and discuss each section, as if it had a separate existence, as if it were independent of its connections and surroundings; or if we do, we necessarily remain in the darkness of error, and, instead of walking in pathways illumined by day, we stumble into pitfalls, we flounder in quagmires concealed by the gloom of night.

Now, few themes, few subjects, are or can be of vaster import than the prosperity and happiness, not only of the twelve millions and more souls dwelling in our Southern land, but of the many more and innumerable millions that are to come after us; and, therefore, there is no question that it behooves us to approach with broader views or with a more judicial spirit. This is not a question that can possibly be handled piece-meal; it cannot be cut up into fragments, but it must be considered in its entirety; or if for convenience it be subdivided, each portion must be considered in reference to every other portion and to the whole.

The student of anatomy necessarily cuts into fragments the human cadaver, but the most important, the most interesting organs—the heart, the lungs, the eyes—are to him but so much unmeaning and useless matter, unless they are studied in connection with every other organ, and with the body as a whole. The story of the members of a man disputing about their relative importance well illustrates this point; each is essential as a part of the whole—all are useless or helpless when taken simply as parts.

It devolves upon a proponent to state his case and to prove it, and this I have sought to do. If, however, I have failed, the failure is owing to the feebleness of the individual rather than to the merits of the subject. But if not only the individual be incompetent, as well I may be in presence of such a theme, but the cause itself be wrong, or even impracticable in the end, my utmost efforts will of course be vain, and I will rejoice in failure, for I have no pride or vanity of any sort to exploit or sustain, and no selfish interest of any kind to subserve. But, right or wrong, a full and free discussion can never injure any good cause, for the maxim is that, when truth and error are free to contend, truth is sure finally to prevail. The individual may and doubtless will be injured in such conflict, but society itself will be the gainer.

But be this as it may, the great question of the prosperity of the South, and all that it implies, is now before the world, and it can be successfully met only by a broad and liberal discussion of the whole merits of the case. We cannot accept some points that are agreeable and reject others that are distasteful unless we can show that what is displeasing is repugnant, and what is pleasing is agreeable to reason itself.

We cannot say that God intends or God never intended so and so, because as yet none of us have been taken into the counsels of the Almighty.

We cannot say that the negro is incapable of elevation, because hitherto under surroundings which have always been adverse to improvement he has done little or nothing for the advancement of civilization, and is still mostly a degraded savage or barbarian, because he has, when exposed to white influences, even those of servitude, greatly improved over his ancestors in Africa, and since freedom he has not only advanced as a race, but particularly as individuals, which we can see before our very eyes.

We cannot say that the South is a white man's country, and that therefore the whites must arbitrarily rule all other colors, even though they be free and equal citizens, for what makes it a white man's country? Does original possession? No; because we robbed the Indians of it and then exterminated them. Does nativity? Yes. Well, the negroes were born here too, and therefore it is as much their country as ours. We cannot say that race prejudice forbids, for granting this kind of prejudice to be almost ineradicable, yet experience and a most elementary knowledge tells us that not only race but also religious prejudice, almost as ineradicable, has been immensely weakened and is still continually wearing away under the influence of reason and commercial intercourse. Humanity has solved many knotty and apparently insoluble questions, and race prejudice, like others, will be solved as well.

We cannot say such things *shall never* be, because can we ever expect to see in the future any greater changes than the present generation has witnessed—from the negro a slave with his life practically in our hands to the negro a law-maker and a juryman sitting in judgment upon the property, yea, and upon the liberty, too, of the former master? and all with our acquiesence.

We cannot say we shall not amend this and cease to do that because others elsewhere do similar things, for this plea (it is not worthy of argument) is worthy only of wayward children, and it condones the reprehensible deeds of others.

We cannot say that the negroes are wretched, poor, degraded, everything that is contemptible and objectionable, for that is but a stronger reason, from the standpoint of prosperity, why we should diligently seek to lift them up and render them thrifty and intelligent, for from nothing nothing can come, and from creatures in their present lowly, degraded and ineffective plight we can expect little or no assistance in our progress towards prosperity.

Yes, we can say and do all the things we ought not to do, and we can leave undone all the things we ought to do—all the power of the United States Government cannot compel us—but in following this course we are making an Ireland of the South, and are digging broad and deep graves in which to bury prosperity and all its untold advantages.

But enough ; the idea is given, and now to the essay.

Richmond, Va., September, 1888.

CONTENTS.

PROSPERITY OF THE SOUTH

DEPENDENT UPON

The Elevation of the Negro.

CHAPTER I.

Prosperity not a free gift of Providence or Chance, but to be bought and full price paid—Is the South Prosperous?

Twenty-odd years ago, when I cast aside the sword and re-entered the walks of civil life, I fondly imagined a great era of prosperity for the South. Guided by history and by a knowledge of our people and our climatic and physical advantages, I saw in anticipation all her tribulations ended, all her scars healed, and all the ravages of war forgotten, and I beheld the South greater, richer and mightier than when she moulded the political policy of the whole country. But year by year these hopes, chastened by experience, have waned and faded, until now, instead of beholding the glorious South of my imagination, I see her sons poorer than when war ceased his ravages, weaker than when rehabilitated with her original rights, and with the bitter memories of the past smouldering, if not rankling, in the bosoms of many.

And why all this great deviation from what was reasonable anticipation? Can it be that some wayward and

(1)

malign providence, actuated by envy, hatred or malice, has guided our ways and efforts to disappointment and disaster, or has chance presided over and wrecked our destiny, or have there been causes of our own or of others, or of nature's making, that have given us stones when we had reason to expect bread?

It cannot be providence, because we cannot suppose that providence is some fortuitous, arbitrary agent, that can be swayed and swerved by prayers and supplications, or by threats and maledictions. Nor can we suppose that providence is a fickle dame, acting on one principle to-day and on the opposite one to-morrow, producing grapes from thorns one season, and figs from thistles the next. On the contrary, providence is strictly just, having no favorites, and holds the scales level between all creatures, regarding neither color, creed, previous condition, nor nationality. Providence is thoroughly realistic, and as thoroughly unsentimental, and smiles and frowns according to acts, and not according to intentions. Providence and justice are linked in close co-partnership, and if things turn not out according to our liking, we may be sure that we and not providence is at fault.

Nor can our disappointment be attributed to chance, blind or otherwise, for there is no such word as chance in religion, or modern philosophy either.

Then our disappointment, if disappointed we are, and our lack of prosperity, if unprosperous we be, must be due to cause. If to cause, then it behooves us to inquire honestly whether it be natural, and therefore irremediable, or artificial and of our own making, and therefore remediable by our own volition, or whether artificial, but of others' making, and therefore remediable only by concert of action. If natural, and therefore beyond our control, we must accommodate ourselves thereto, for nature never consults man's convenience. If of our own making, and therefore remediable, it doubly behooves us to remove all such cause. But if of others' making, but yet remediable, it likewise behooves us to look around and seek for such removal too. Doubtless all these causes conspire more or less towards our lack of prosperity, but it is of the causes within our own control that we are now mainly concerned, and the others will not be touched.

The real question before us is: Is the South prosperous? If the correct answer be in the affirmative, then this proposed inquiry is altogether fruitless; but if in the negative, then this proposed inquiry into the prosperity of the South becomes the most momentous that can engage our attention. Judging by the glowing reports in the newspapers for the past three years, we must conclude that the South is enjoying a veritable deluge of prosperity, and that both individually and as States they are surpassing even the Eastern States, those petted children of legislation since the foundation of the Union. Judging by these sheets, one would naturally imagine that the South is a region where poverty is unknown and where everybody is industriously and successfully laying up wealth; where manufacturing sites are engrossing arable lands; where cotton, so long king, is tottering on his throne, and where manufactures are about to usurp his sceptre. Seen through newspaper lenses, the South is indeed a happy Acadia.

Just here it may be well to say a few words about so-called Manufacturers' Records which are circulating a vast amount of misinformation about the growth and prosperity of the South, and misleading multitudes on this point.

Such journals proceed on the same plan as would the Superintendent of the Census in 1890, should he, instead of actually enumerating the people, start with the population of 1880, and add thereto not only all the births, but also all the still-births, all the miscarriages, and all the abortions since that year, and deduct nothing for deaths in the meanwhile. Of course such a computation would be utterly absurd, and could only lead to ridiculous conclusions. But so it is with the computations of the so-called Manufacturers' Records. In arriving at their aggregates of additional manufactures they write to the proprietors of every scheme they see noticed in their local exchanges, and they include not only concerns that have actually begun operations, but also all projected, and even all suggested enterprises, all of which they capitalize at the highest authorized amount, and to make their calculations all the more mischievous and misleading they deduct nothing for the many hundreds or many thousands of manufacturing concerns that annually fail or retire from business.

Thus in the census of 1880 the South is credited with $133,240,000 manufacturing capital, but for the last eight years these reliable records have by actual, probable, and possible manufacturing enterprises, by capitalizing them at their maximum and by deducting nothing for failures and retirements, added not less than $1,000,000,000 to the manufacturing capital of the South, or nearly eight times as much as the South started with in 1865, and had succeeded in gathering together during the subsequent fifteen years. The impression is sought to be conveyed that while the South had $133,240,000 employed in manufactures in 1880 she has in 1888 $1,133,240,000 so employed.* This is entirely false, because the South has lost since 1880 quite as much as she has gained in manufactures, or at the very best no one at all familiar with the South doubts that the census will show no greater increase of manufactures than it does population. The writer lives in one of the principal manufacturing cities of the

---

*Thus the Baltimore Manufacturer's Record of March 29th, 1889, reports for first Quarter of 1889 an addition of $12,162,0C0 to the manufacturing capital of the eleven Southern States.

South, and he observes therein no great increase of manufactures, the failures having almost if not quite offset the increase. In the mineral regions there has been some increase, but it is pretty certain that this growth has been fully offset by decadence in the South at large.

Newspaper compilations may discredit such opinions, but while such compilations are praiseworthy in intent, we all know what exaggerations they usually are when confronted by official documents. They are generally based upon "about" statements of the parties applied to, and in such cases "about" generally means largely in excess of the actual, just as current rumor reports A or B to be worth "about" one or ten millions, when the executor is glad to find half the "about." Thus in Richmond, the *Dispatch's* compilation of manufactures for 1879 was $23,466,640, while according to the census of 1880, six months later, they were $20,790,000, and the population January 1, 1880, was 80,000 according to the board of health, while the census, taken five months later, gave a population of 63,600.

A few words also as to the glowing reports of the prosperity of the South as set forth by Colonel Alex. K. McClure, Hon. Wm. D. Kelly, and others. These gentlemen occupy pretty much the position of kings who, surrounded by ministers and courtiers whose interest it is to keep them in darkness, rarely if ever know the true state of affairs, and their opinions are of as little value. These gentlemen who undertake to learn the condition of affairs by a hurried trip in palace cars are usually taken in charge and coached by interested parties, who carry them to a few selected spots like Birmingham and Chattanooga, where there is much life, activity and growth, and are told exultingly, "There! Look! Does not this remind you of Pennsylvania?" &c., &c. These gentlemen are thus placed in the attitude of envoys in olden times to an enemy's camp. The envoys were led blindfolded through the camp, and their eyes were only unbandaged when they reached the royal headquarters, where everything had been prearranged to impress them with the power and magnificence of the army or sovereign. So these gentlemen, having been hurried through hundreds of miles in luxurious palace coaches, have practically been blindfolded as to the condition of the country passed through, and not having their eyes unbandaged until in the midst of furnaces, rolling-mills, and all the activities of a manufacturing centre, they are dazzled by what they see, and they at once jump to the conclusion that what they behold is merely a type of the whole South, and that as there is great prosperity before their eyes, so there is great prosperity in the South.

These gentlemen altogether forget, most likely, listening to the brilliant conversation of their chaperones about the new South; have not seen the hundreds and hundreds of miles of poor country passed through, with its fenceless plantations, its unpainted and dilapidated homesteads, its small proportion of cultivated fields and its large proportion of lands returning and returned to a state of nature, its patches instead of its fields of crops, the scarcity of stock of all kinds, and the thriftless and idle groups found at almost every depot. They lose sight of the real South—that is to say, of ninety-five per cent. thereof, but seeing the other five per cent. concentrated in two or three active, stirring, and busy cities they erroneously conclude that the ninety-five per cent. which they do not and cannot see is like the five per cent. which they have been invited to inspect. Reversing the process of the tiny fragment held close to the eye, hiding the sun and holding these bits of sunshine close to the eye, the South at large, great though its poverty actually is, is made to appear as bright and as prosperous as these bits of sunshine.

If, instead of this process, these gentlemen would visit the farming and planting community, whether cotton,

tobacco, sugar, grain, or what not be raised, which is the
real South, and if they were brought into actual business
contact with the people themselves they would soon see,
even leaving out the six millions of negroes who are in
the depths of indigence, that fully ninety-five per cent. of
the whites would at death leave their families, after debts
were paid, with scarcely more than a roof to cover them
and that for every ten living in any degree of ease and
comfort there were ninety who had nothing beyond the
commonest necessaries of life.   Yes, there shall be a new
South, and prominent men from the North must be
brought to testify to it, even though their testimony must
in the nature of the case be untrustworthy and valueless.

To doubt is to be damned, is true in other things
besides religion, and so to doubt the current charming
presentations of Southern growth and prosperity is to bring
down anathemas upon one's head.   What! the South not
prosperous.   Impossible, they cry; and the individual who
questions is an idiot.

Would that the South were rich, because numberless
blessings follow in the train of wealth, just as numberless
evils follow in the trail of poverty.   To be rich is to be
great, mighty and powerful, to be feared, honored and
respected like the United States, like Great Britain, like
Germany; to be poor is to be weak, wretched and miserable, to be despised, plundered and imposed upon, like
Spain, Turkey, or Mexico.   If claiming to be rich made
the South rich, none could make louder or more vehement
claims than myself, and a rejuvenated giant South should
ever be on my tongue; but claims and boasts are vain in
the face of nature, which demands deeds and not sentiments, but deeds in accordance with principles of well-
established economic laws.

Prosperity is an inestimable blessing, and to obtain it
we must, like the husbandman in Scripture who sold
everything to purchase one field, make every sacrifice,

and be deterred by no difficulties; but like all other good things prosperity has its price, and we must pay the full price or must go without, and the greater the good the greater the cost. We all desire prosperity, and we have been sighing for it for years, and yet prosperity lingers; but if we have it not it is because we have not sought aright—that is, not in accordance with the laws of nature.

In order for success one must understand fully his position as well as be willing to take all necessary steps to secure success, for his measures cannot be appropriate if this knowledge be lacking.

So in the following pages I will, in order to do my mite towards placing the South in the proud and influential position she should occupy, endeavor to set forth first, her actual condition and conspiring causes; and second, I will seek to point out the steps necessary to be taken in order to attain prosperity. In doing the first, I will not draw for facts upon irresponsible newspapers, but upon United States official documents, mainly those of the census of 1880, or upon other sources which are universally recognized as authorities. The principal cause thereof—namely, the degradation of the negro—will be set forth at length, but candidly and plainly, so that if possible others may see as I do, or so that the resulting discussion may clear my vision and that of others seeing as I do.

In doing the second, the remedies will require greater, space, but they will be treated in the same plain, candid and fair manner as in discussing the condition and cause thereof of the South; and all will be done solely with a view to letting us see ourselves as we really are, so that perceiving clearly what is essential to be done, and being willing to do it, we may attain our longed-for prosperity, the one thing needful for our happiness as individuals, and for our greatness as States.

Chapter II.

South not Prosperous—Why?—Principal Cause Degradation of the Negro—Elevation of the Negro Urged on Economic Grounds, not on Grounds of Justice or Religion.

As many streams are required to make the river, so many causes are required to produce prosperity, and as the river is great in proportion to the number of streams flowing together, so prosperity is great in proportion to the number of causes harmoniously co-operating.

There are many causes conspiring to the poverty or lack of prosperity of the South, the principal of which are a General Prevalence of Ignorance—a General Disregard of Human Life—a General Lack of Economy and Self-denial; but great as these causes are, a greater and more far-reaching cause of all is the Degradation of the Negro, who, being our principal source of labor, is our principal dependence for prosperity.

Each of these causes would greatly retard the prosperity of the South, or indeed of any country, but all of them combined, destructive as they would necessarily be to prosperity, are not as serious and as fatal as the last cause, namely: The Degradation of the Negro. Like a malignant cancer which poisons the whole system, this degradation seems to intensify all the other drawbacks under which we labor. Thus general ignorance is intensified by the gross ignorance of all the blacks and of the whites nearest them in social and financial condition; the general disregard of human life is intensified by the slight regard in which a negro's life is held, and the whites, regarding the negro's life of little sanctity, naturally regard all life as of little value, and therefore freely take each other's life; and the general lack of economy and self-denial is naturally intensified by the careless, wasteful and negligent manner in which the negro, upon whom we are mainly dependent for labor, usually does his work.   The negro is an extremely defective tool, and no man, whether planter, carpenter, or what not, can continue constantly to use wretched implements without becoming wasteful and negligent himself, and without disregarding economy.   We may remove all the other hindrances to prosperity; the whites may become well educated; we may hold human life in scrupulous regard and may become models of economy and self-denial, but if the blacks are to be left to grovel in their present degraded condition, even then prosperity would be measurably in default, because the six million negroes, remaining degraded, would prove an incubus upon the whites, who would be in imminent danger of impoverishment by the thieving of such multitudes, whose highest and only ambition would be to live without work at the expense of those who were responsible for their degradation.   But then let education be generally disseminated among the whites as it is in some of the other States, let human life be as well protected as in a really civilized community— England, for example—and let economy and self-denial prevail as in the New England States, the elevation of the negro would follow as a matter of course, or rather it would go along *pari passu* with the elevation of the whites themselves, and his degradation as a race would become a matter of history.

Although justice—and we should always bear in mind that justice is a stern virtue that will sooner or later avenge herself upon her violators, though at the same time she never fails to honor and reward those who respect her requirements—although justice demands that the whites elevate the negroes, for in the light of morality we stand responsible for their welfare, their elevation will not be advocated on any such ground, nor on the ground of religion either, but simply on economic grounds, on the ground of advantage to the whites. Just as we would urge the South to improve its animals, tools, methods of planting, &c., so that they may derive the more good from their labor and capital, so we urge the elevation of the negro, because the better men and citizens they are the more we, the whites, can in the end make out of them.

That is very hard doctrine, perhaps, but we must remember that facts themselves are hard things, and that they never think of accommodating themselves to either our desires or our fancies. We would like a more "comforting" (as the women would say) doctrine, did not reading, observation and experience show that morality and even religion are very poor advocates, unless they can sh ow to their listeners that material benefit is on their side. Convinced, therefore, as I must be that benefit is the only safe and sound ground to base an argument upon ; for if a thing does not benefit or afford us pleasure in some way, how can it interest us? I shall address all my arguments to prove not only that the prosperity of the South will be increased by, but that it is dependent upon, the elevation of the negro, and if it is not so shown, then this effort will be in vain, and if it cannot be so shown, then all effort to elevate the negro will be in vain. If the southern people cannot be shown that his elevation is for their interest, then the negro must forever grovel, but if it is demonstrated as we go along that his elevation is essential to our welfare, then as sensible people we should throw aside the thickly-incrusted prepossessions or prejudices of centuries and hasten the day when we shall have made the negro a free man (for as long as he labors under any but natural disabilities he is little better than a serf), and therefore a worthy and competent co-worker in the race for prosperity, which we have long seen through a glass darkly, but which, like an *ignis fatuus*, has eluded our grasp, and which will continue to as long as the negro is degraded and without hope of rising above his present status—a status of perpetual inferiority and subordination.

In discussing this question, which is the gravest and most momentous confronting the South, now happily mostly local, but which before long will become national if the South proves herself incapable or unwilling to solve it, I shall set forth—first, the material condition of the South, drawn from well-established sources, which will be seen to be one of great poverty—certainly of comparative poverty; and, second, after showing the state of education I will point out at greater length the steps which are necessary to convert, by elevating the negro, this poverty into prosperity.

It may seem both invidious and presumptuous to attempt this *role*, but while frankly admitting that I may be presumptuous, my Southern ancestry, birth, rearing, residence and interest preserve me from the charge of invidiousness; but if my directing attention to the poverty and illiteracy of the South be thought by many to be unpatriotic, or if my opposition to our present undemocratic condition of affairs be considered treasonable, I will then patiently bear the odium attached to such charges.

CHAPTER III.

South not Prosperous—Example of Georgia—Her Poverty—Contrary Example of Palatinate in 1674—Few or no Savings Banks—Few other Banks—Proportion of Railways—Very Few Manufactures and they very Crude—Statistics Thereof—Production of Iron and Steel in 1887—Manufactures of Thirteen Southern Cities—Summary of Aggregated Wealth.

That the South ought to be the richest section of the United States goes without saying, for it occupies not only a broad and fertile territory, but it lies beneath a sun that produces in abundance many of the most valuable productions of commerce. In addition to the great staff of life—bread—tobacco and cotton flourish here as nowhere else, and rice, sugar, and naval stores add millions annually to its wealth, but although this production has been going on uninterruptedly for more than twenty years her people are not rich, but on the contrary are very poor. They are not only burdened with debt up to their full capacity for borrowing, but much, if not the greatest part, of their crops is made by loans, beginning with the time of planting. Their homes are not only unsupplied with many of the most essential comforts, but their plantations are ill supplied with stock and implements, their cribs and smokehouses are mostly empty, their fences have disappeared, and their dwellings and farm-buildings are not only indifferent, but they present a general appearance of neglect and too often of dilapidation. The want of accumulated capital is extreme, and for at least six months of the year money, instead of being a reality, is rather a thing of memory and of hope, or of the past and the future, with the greater part of the people. But as an ounce of prevention is worth a pound of cure, so well-attested facts, even though they be few, are worth libraries of speculations and assertion, we will therefore bid adieu to assertions which are of no authority, and will resort to facts to substantiate our statements.

We have all heard of Georgia, of her great progress and prosperity; and as she has been held up as a model to all the other States, we of the South have come to recognize her authority on both material and moral matters with the utmost reverence and humility; we can therefore all rely upon what Georgia does and says. We will, then, refer to Georgia, and trust what she says regarding the material condition of her people, and her Comptroller-General, in his annual report for the year ending September 30th, 1886, shall be the spokesman.

But before proceeding to the analysis of this report, let us remark that it was made twenty years after the close of the war, in which Georgia was not specially scourged except along the line of Sherman's march. Let us also remark that Turenne in 1674 devastated the Palatinate to such a degree that in the language of General Sheridan "a crow flying across it was compelled to carry his rations," even the fruit trees and the vines being destroyed, yet twenty years thereafter scarcely a trace of her horrible devastation was visible. Now, bearing further in mind that this report was made twenty years after the war, we will expect to find that Georgia had repaired her ravages quite as well as had the pauper labor of the Palatinate. According to the report, we find the following condition of wealth:

Assessed value of personal property.			. $123,141,286 00
"	"	per capita, adding 15 per cent. increase from 1880 to 1886 . . .	70 00
"	"	per capita—whites	124 47
"	"	" " —negroes	6 54
"	"	whites—household and kitchen furniture ·	12 30

Assessed value	whites—plantation and mechanical tools		$ 5 65
"	"	whites—live stock all kinds . .	24 58
"	"	negroes—live stock all kinds .	2 60
"	"	negroes—plantation and mechanical tools	31
"	"	negroes—household and kitchen furniture	1 03

Personal property is taken because real estate remaining substantially the same is not, in agricultural communities, subject to much change of value.

Now reflect for a moment. Here are people laboring for twenty years, and granted they began with *no* personal property, they have gathered wealth at the annual rate per head of $3.50, or at the rate of $6.18 for the whites; and counting a family as five persons, each family has accumulated annually $17.50, or $30.90 for each white family. But this is on the supposition that everybody started as they came into the world—with not a rag to their back, with not a chair, table or bed, with not a pan, plate or dish, with not a wagon, plow or hoe, with not a horse, cow or hog—in fact, with nothing. But as it is scarcely possible to conceive of a respectable white family without at least $61.50 of household and kitchen furniture, or of a plantation without at least $28.25 of implements and tools, or without $123 of live stock of all kinds, one fairly good mule being worth that, it is not unreasonable to affirm that the people of Georgia had not added materially to their wealth during the twenty years preceding 1886.

But it has been claimed that the negroes of Georgia have also prospered very much. What does the report say? The negroes at least began with no accumulated property. According to the report each colored family possessed in 1886 an average of $5.13 of household and kitchen furniture, of $1.55 of mechanical and farming implements, and of $13 of live stock of all kinds.

Truly prosperity ran riot with the colored brother, and,

being so wealthy, it is not surprising that we have the pretty general complaint that the negro is lazy and wont work.

If we find no prosperity in Georgia it will be vain to look for it in the other Southern States, and we will not, therefore, adduce any more statistics, although they are to hand in abundance. But granting prosperity for the whites, who can deny that the blacks, who comprise forty per cent. of the population, are in the very depths of poverty, and therefore of degradation; for poverty and degradation are always twin sisters, and that if anything has been done to elevate them the attempt has been a lamentable failure. Leaving now individual let us come to general or aggregate wealth, a few particulars of which must, for want of space, suffice. And first—

SAVINGS BANKS.

In settled countries where the land has been cleared, fences made and houses built, if there is any, certainly if there is much prosperity, money will accumulate, and it will find its way into savings banks, and cause their formation if there are none or not enough already exist. In new States like Florida, Texas and Arkansas, savings banks may not be expected, because prosperous people can find better uses for their money in buying lands and opening new farms than in putting it in savings banks. But in the other eight Southern States, where land is all appropriated, the accumulations that follow thrift would almost certainly find their way into savings banks, and if savings banks do not appear and flourish, it may be accepted as infallible evidence that there is little or no prosperity. Now what do we find. The United States Comptroller of the Treasury in his report for 1885–'6 reports:

	Deposits in Savings Banks.
Southern States	. . . .
All other States	$1,141,530,578 00

There were doubtless some few savings banks in the South, but none to attract the attention of an official, who is himself a southerner.

Banks are another evidence of prosperity, for the accumulations of prosperity naturally seek investment in banks. The following is the report of United States Comptroller of the Currency, December 4, 1886:

	So. States.	Other States.
Capital stock paid in	$31,065,450 00	$517,175,280 00
Surplus fund	8,262,139 00	148,987,051 00
Undivided profits	4,483,274 00	62,020,200 00
Total	$43,810,863 00	$728,182,551 00

Banks are not only evidences of prosperity, but they are in turn causes of prosperity. What shall we say, then, of the prosperity of the South when it possesses six per cent. of banking capital for twenty-six per cent. of population?

Railroads are also an index of wealth, and what is their testimony? The highest authority (Poor's R. R. Manual for 1886) reports:

	So. States.	All other States.
Total investments	$1,108,428,000	$7,230,858,000

This is a better showing than in savings banks and banks, for it is thirteen per cent. to twenty-six per cent. of population. But this showing is delusive, because it is well known that almost all southern roads have been built with northern capital, and that not five per cent. of the total of $1,108,428,000 is owned in the South. Except as occupying southern soil and as sources of taxation, railroads are scarcely more southern in origin and ownership than if they were located in one of the planets.

Manufactures are other evidences of wealth, and what is their report? Here we have to go back some years to the United States census of 1880, but this evidence will

probably be demurred to by devout believers in a New
South, for they will say manufactures have made wonderful strides since then. Such objectors may be correct,
but it is extremely doubtful, because except in Birmingham, Chattanooga and a few other localities an observer
can behold few material evidences of increase of manufactures; certainly nothing commensurate with the
growth of manufactures in most of the other States. The
last census reports: Manufactures in the South, $240,-
444,295; in all other, $5,129,223,411; which is not quite
five per cent., against twenty-six per cent. of population.
Bearing in mind that southern manufactures were mostly
of the coarsest character, requiring the least skill, and
therefore earning the least profit, the poverty of the South
under this head is all the more striking and lamentable;
and to show this, the following digest is made from the
report:

ELEVEN SOUTHERN STATES.

Cotton manufactures..	16,165,607
Woolen manufactures	2,336,597
Flour and grist mills	63,803,041
Foundry products	7,091,959
Iron and steel products	7,836,653
Lumber products. . . . . · . .	31,620,878
Naval stores	5,871,983
Tobacco . . . . , . . .	20,138,340

$154,865,058

Observe that $63,803,041 are credited to flour and
grist mills, which are mostly small neighborhood affairs,
and most of this amount is as fairly credited to manufactures as if we credited to bakeries the subsequent
labors of the women in converting the flour and the meal
into loaf-bread, biscuits, ashcake and pone. To the credit
of lumber is passed $31,620,878. This is one of the
crudest of manufactures, and instead of classing saw-mills
under the head of wealth-producers, we should rather
class them under the head of bankruptcy-breeders. Only

$13,502,224 go to the credit of textiles, and only $14,928,612 to iron and steel and their varied products.

The difference, according to census, between cost of manufactures and what the manufactures sell for is twenty per cent. Therefore, in the census year seventy-four per cent. of population added about $1,000,000,000 to their wealth, while the twenty-six per cent. of Southern population added only $48,000,000.

This was in 1880, and probably we may hear a chorus of " patriotic " Southerners and enthusiastic believers in a new South scornfully exclaim, " 1880! oh, yes, 1880 ! " and most probably these gentlemen will exclaim : " Talk at this stage of the world, when the South is taking such giant strides, of 1880; you had as well talk to us about the time when Captain John Smith was having his romantic adventure with old Powhatan and his lovely Pocahontas.

But although we have no late census to refer to, we have official figures of the iron industry, the one in which the South is said to have accomplished most, so let us see what these figures say :

	1880.		
	South.	Whole Country.	Percentage.
	Tons.	Tons.	South.
Production Pig Iron	207,798	1,295,411	5
	1887.		
Production Pig Iron . . .	767,791	7,187,206	10
Production Steel, all kinds . . .		3,739,760	0

Here is a wonderful progress, worthy of being cele-brated with a full band of jewsharps. Here is the South with enough coal and iron, almost locked in each others embrace, to supply the world with iron at the very lowest cost, and yet in seven years she has added 560,000 tons to her product, or an additional five per cent. on the total production of the whole country. While the South was adding 560.000 tons the rest of the country added 2,900,000 tons. Observe that the South is not credited with a pound of the 3,739,760 tons of steel produced in 1887.

The census of 1880 gives in minute detail the manufactures of over one hundred principal cities and the following summary is presented: Thirteen southern cities, total manufactures, $77,191,000, of which

Richmond manufactured		$ 20,790,030
New Orleans	"	18,808,000
Nashville	"	8,597,000
Atlanta	"	4,862,000
Memphis	"	4,415,000

As a comparison the following is interesting:

New York manufactured		$ 472,926,000
Philadelphia	"	324,345,000
Chicago	"	249,023,000
Brooklyn	"	177,220,000
Boston	"	130,532,000
St. Louis	"	114,833,000
Cincinnati	"	105,259,000
Pittsburgh	"	75,915,000

It will be observed that New York city manufactured about twice as much as the whole South, and Chicago as much, and when the grade of manufactures of the two sections is considered, the comparison will be all the more striking. Note, also, that Pittsburgh manufactured nearly as much as thirteen principal southern cities.

" Patriotism " would say hide all these uncomplimentary facts, but common sense says it is better to look our deficiencies squarely in the face, for we will never overcome our shortcomings until we are convinced of their existence. Common sense beats "patriotism" every time, and while things frequently go backwards under the lead of " patriotism," which is only a longer word for " gush," they are always pushing forward under the guidance of common sense. " Know thyself " is not only essential for the individual, but also for the State.

At the close of this branch of our subject we condense our facts into a summary, so that we may see our condition at a glance.

EXHIBIT OF INDIVIDUAL WEALTH.

Value per head personal property in Georgia		$ 70 00
" " for whites	$ 124 47	
" " for blacks	6 54	
" " household and kitchen furniture, whites .	12 30	
" " " " " " blacks .	1 03	
" " farm and mechanical tools, whites	5 65	
" " " " " " blacks	31	
" " live stock, all kinds, whites	24 58	
" " " " " blacks	2 60	

EXHIBIT OF AGGREGATE WEALTH.

SOURCES.	South.	Other States.	Per Cent. of Southern Population.	Per Cent. South.
Savings Banks. . . .	. . . . . .	1,141,530,578	26	. .
National Banks . . .	43,810,863	728,182,551	26	6
State B'ks and bankrs	very little	nearly all	26	trace
Telegraph stock . . .	nothing	all	26	. .
L. F. & M. Ins. stocks	very little	nearly all	26	trace
Vessel property . . .	very little	nearly all	26	trace
Manufactures, 1880 .	240,444,495	5,129,223,411	26	5
Pig Iron, 1880—tons .	207,798	4,097,616	26	5
Pig Iron, 1887—tons .	767,791	6,419,515	26	10
Steel, 1887—tons. . .	. . . . . .	3,739,760	26	. .
Railroads	1,108,428,000	7,230,858,000	26	13

CHAPTER IV.

GROWTH OF THE CITIES.

Growth of Cities and Causes Thereof—Examples—Growth of Thirty Southern Cities and of Four Ohio and Four New Jersey Cities.

But the optimists, though staggered probably by the preceding unfavorable statistics, will, in proof of their claim of the great progress and prosperity of the South, point triumphantly to the growth of the cities.

Well, granting all claimed, what does it amount to, unless it can be shown that the growth of the cities is the outgrowth of the prosperity of the farming and rural districts, for it by no means follows that growth of cities always means the prosperity of the State? Generally, perhaps, growth of cities means prosperity of the State, but sometimes it means decay. In the case of England and Scotland their fifty-three cities, ranging in population by census of 1881 from 50,762 to 3,832,441, means prosperity, but the twenty-four cities of Italy (census 1881), ranging in population from 50,651 to 494,314, and the fifteen cities of Spain (census 1877), ranging from 49,855 to 397,-690, does not mean either prosperity or progress, for both Italy and Spain are extremely poor, backward and stagnant.

There are other causes than prosperity to promote the growth of cities. Decay also promotes their growth, or at least temporarily, and cities sometimes linger long after the country is dead. Constantinople was a populous city long after the Eastern Empire was a mere shadow, and Constantinople is still a populous city, although the Ottoman Empire has been moribund the last one hundred years.

In a declining or decaying State, with agriculture on the wane and social order disturbed, there is a constant influx into the cities—where there is more life and activity, more society, and especially more security. In such a State, the younger and more ambitious desert the villages and the country because they have a lessening field for their energies; professional men of all kinds do the same; families of means and culture, tiring of a country life constantly becoming harder and more unsocial, follow next; then follow the timid, who dread the relaxations of legal restraint upon the improvident and badly disposed, and then those seeking the advantages of education which constantly diminish in such a State. And along with what may be termed the higher classes, the mechanical and laboring people who find work becoming scarcer, and wages smaller and more uncertain, also flock to the cities where, if anywhere, employment is to be had. And thus it is that cities grow in decaying countries.

Now, most of these causes of increase of our cities have been operating for the past twenty years, and they have not yet exhausted their forces. Thousands and tens of thousands, yea hundreds of thousands, of our most cultured and refined people have deserted their ancestral homes and have settled in Southern cities and elsewhere in the United States, and few or none have taken their places. The writer knows of neighborhoods that have been deserted almost *en masse* by their former wealthy inhabitants, and plantations, where twenty years ago negroes were to be found by the four score, are now almost tenantless wastes. And let any city resident of twenty years' standing inquire who his neighbors and acquaintances are, and he will be astonished at the numbers who have within that time from some one of the foregoing causes emigrated from the country; and let any housekeeper inquire into the origin of the servants he employs, and he will find that fully half are country-bred. But the city's gain has been the country's loss, for few have taken the places of those who have turned their backs upon their birthplaces and family burying-grounds.

But have our cities really increased much in population? Let us see. But, unfortunately, in order to do so, we must go back to antiquity—namely, the census of 1880—for this authority will be repudiated by the optimists of these modern days—to-wit: the year of grace, 1888. They will claim enormous gains since 1880, and they are doubtless correct as to a considerable increase in many instances; but when we remember how easy it is to make claims when no proof is demanded, or when no disproof is ready at hand, we should not be surprised at the great claims of increase that every city makes, and discount them accordingly. There is among the denizens of every city—and we might say of every village, too—a sense of personal responsibility for the growth of such place; there is a feeling of pride if the place is thought to be growing, and of mortification if it is thought to be stationary, or even growing slowly, and in order to nourish their pride and to conceal their mortification, they all naturally fall into the habit of exaggerating the growth of their city, town, or village. If the place of their residence is found by accurate census to have grown and to be still growing rapidly, so that it outstrips other cities that they had been jealous of, then a regular *civis Romanus sum* feeling takes possession of them, and they brag, and strut, and bluster, as if they had performed some great deeds. Who does not remember the general dissatisfaction with the last census when it failed to show such growth as localities and cities had fondly claimed?

But here is what the census of 1880 says as to the growth of the thirty principal Southern cities:

	Pop. in 1880.	Inc. 1870 to 1880.
Alexandria.	13,659	89
Atlanta	37,409	15,620
Augusta	21,891	6,592
Chattanooga.	12,892	6,799
Charleston	49,984	1,028
Columbus, Ga.	10,123	2,722
Columbia	10,036	738
Galveston	22,248	8,430
Greenville, S. C.	6,160	2,409
Jackson, Miss	5,204	970
Jacksonville	7,650	738
Knoxville	9,663	1,013
Little Rock.	13,105	758
Lynchburg.	15,959	9,134
Macon.	12,749	1,939
Montgomery.	16,713	6,125
Nashville.	43,350	17,485
New Orleans	216,090	24,672
Norfolk	21,966	2,737
Petersburg	21,656	2,706
Portsmouth.	13,390	800
Richmond	63,600	12,562
Raleigh.	9,265	1,475
Savannah	30,709	2,474
San Antonio	20,550	8,430
Wilmington, N. C.	17,350	3,904
Total		142,259

From which deduct the decrease in the following cities during the same decade—

Memphis.	33,592	6,634
Mobile.	29,132	2,902
Natchez	7,058	1,999
Vicksburg.	11,814	629
Total		12,164

—and we have a net increase in the growth of the thirty principal Southern cities of 130,095.

2

Compare this growth with that of the four Ohio cities:

Increase 1870 to 1880.

Cincinnati	38,900
Columbus	20,373
Cleveland	67,316
Toledo	18,533
	145,122

or with that of the four Jersey cities:

Camden	21,604
Jersey City	38,176
Newark	47,929
Paterson	29,694
	137,403

In view of these *facts,* will it not seem amusing to speak of the growth and prosperity of the South? And even this increase is partially delusive, because the census of 1870 was taken when political affairs were very much out of joint, when the work was committed to ignorant and careless hands, and was therefore very imperfectly done.

Chapter V.

SOME OF THE CAUSES OF THIS LACK OF PROSPERITY.

Why Elevate the Negro? To make Him an Efficient and Profitable Wealth-Producer—Must Trample or Must Elevate—Must make him a Slave or a Man—Labor Corner-Stone of Wealth. Examples of No-Worker, of Unintelligent Worker, and of Intelligent Worker—South can expect Prosperity only through Intelligent Labor—United States would still be a Wilderness but for Intelligent Labor.

Having sufficiently demonstrated, it is thought, not only the comparative, but also the positive, poverty of the South, which ought in many respects to be the richest section, let us now proceed to point out some of the causes of this poverty, or at all events of this want of prosperity.

As already stated, these causes are many, the chief of which are illiteracy, disregard of human life, lack of economy and self-denial, and degradation of the negro—already mentioned, and vicious economic legislation, one of the most insidious, because generally unsuspected, of all the causes sapping our prosperity. For want of space only one of these causes will be treated, except incidentally, but as this cause is the greatest of all, and in a measure underlies all but the last cause, by handling this cause properly, the whole field affecting our prosperity will have been gone over, and this cause is the degradation of the negro.

But the question really to be considered, is not the degradation of the negro, for that is patent to all, but

the elevation of the negro, for it is by his elevation alone
that we are to secure prosperity, for elevate him and the
other evils will be cured during the process of his elevation.

But the question will be very generally asked, Why
elevate the negro at all?   Is he not now good enough to
obey us obsequiously, and to make our corn, our cotton,
our tobacco, our rice, and our sugar?   What more do we
want of him?   The reply is that if the negro is forever
to remain simply the instrument for doing our menial
and manual work, for ploughing and sewing, for driving
mules, for worming tobacco and picking cotton, he is
already too elevated, and he should be still further hum-
bled and degraded.   In his present condition he has some
of the ideas and aspirations of a freeman, some desires for
education, and he has almost entire control of his personal movements.   He works when it suits him, but then
he may idle at the crisis of a crop; but as we cannot compel him with the lash to work, he is on the whole neither
a profitable laborer for himself nor for an employer.   To
make him efficient, and to make him work the crop at
the proper time, in spite of the attractions of political
and religious gatherings, the overseer with the lash must
be ever before his eyes.   To allow the negro to remain as
he is, is for him a still "lower deep" in the social scale,
and in his descent he drags us down with him.

But if the negro is to become an intelligent voter, is
to be a citizen capable of taking a sensible part in the
affairs of his community, and to be a valuable co-worker
in adding to the wealth of the State, then we have a vast
deal to do in order to elevate him.   To make him *our*
assistant in the production of wealth, the negro must be
made to work, or he must be induced by ambition, by
the hope of enjoying in full the fruits of his labors, to
work steadily and intelligently.   If we are not willing to
elevate him, we should set to work resolutely and delib-

erately to manacle both his mind and limbs, and to cow
him, so that a little white child shall control a thousand.
We will then at least get enough out of him to supply
his few physical wants and to enable us to live in idle-
ness and comparative comfort, which is not now the case.
But if there is no hope of our ever being able to do this,
what is the next best thing for us to do for our own good?
Make a man of him. But this can be done only by
means of education and other fostering influences, by cultivating his self-respect, by inspiring his hope, by letting
him see that the land of his birth is as much his country as it is of the wealthiest and haughtiest white. Now
he is not only an alien, but an inferior—in reality a serf,
in the land of his nativity.

We must trample, or we must elevate; to maintain the
status quo is impossible. To trample is to perpetuate and
intensify the poverty and stagnation under which we
groan; to elevate is to make the South rich, happy and
strong.

To say that labor is the corner-stone—yea, the whole
foundation too, of wealth—is merely to utter a truism, but
how few of us, while freely acknowledging, actually realize
this fact. For example: Place a man and his family in
a Garden of Eden, where fruits, ripening the year round,
abound on every hand, and where the climate requires
slight clothing and shelter, and suppose none of them
labor. If they had been supplied with tools, house and
garments, in a few years at furthest, they would be
naked, toolless and houseless, for these things wear out or
decay; or if they had not been supplied with these things
they would, not laboring, at the end of ten, fifty or a
thousand years be the same helpless, useless animals they
were when first created.

But suppose this family, willing to work and anxious to
improve their condition; but suppose through ignorance
they do not know how to avail themselves of the forces

of nature; or suppose they misapplied the little knowledge they did gain through painful experience, at the end
of ten, fifty or a thousand years, they would not be greatly
better off, and though increased in numbers, the family
would most probably be like, and no further advanced
than were the Indians, when our ancestors landed and
began to rob them of their homes and patrimony. This
family was industrious, but not intelligent.

But suppose this same family, not only willing to work
and anxious to improve their condition, but intelligent
also; inquisitive of nature, and availing themselves of the
forces of air and water in their various applications, and
prying into the laws of mechanics and inventing wea-
pons, tools, vehicles, &c., &c., then at the end of twenty
years this family will have made considerable advance in
their condition; at the end of a century or two it will
have grown into a barbarous tribe of some size and
importance, and at the end of a millenium it will have
developed into a wealthy and powerful kingdom.

By this simple, though perhaps needless, illustration,
we may clearly see that not merely labor, but intelligent
labor, is the sole basis of prosperity, and that prosperity
is proportionate to the intelligence of labor. This is,
however, merely preliminary to saying that the South is
no exception to this universal truth, and that she, like all
other countries, can expect prosperity only in proportion
to the intelligence of her laborers. And by intelligence
is not meant simply book-learning, for frequently those
deeply versed in books are learned, but they are far from
being intelligent; but by intelligence is meant a certain
alertness of perception which enables one to grasp the
situation or business in hand so as to avoid the difficulties or hindrances presented, and to appropriate the
advantages offered. And by laborers is not meant simply those who dig and plough and who do the manual
work of society, but also those who think, plan and
direct.

Thus the first agriculturists being ignorant could devise no better aid than a sharp, hard stick for stirring the soil, but intelligence aiding, they followed this with a spade made of the shoulder-blade of some wild beast; this was followed by a forked limb drawn by a domestic animal, but intelligence has not ceased her efforts, although science and skill seem to have reached perfection in the modern plow. And this same holds true with spinning, weaving, sewing, locomotion, &c., &c.—in almost everything intelligent labor has, as it were, evolved the mighty oak out of the tiny acorn. Intelligent labor has converted the Western wilderness into great and populous States, to which the sceptre of empire is being fast transferred; and labor, lacking in intelligence, has left the South, with all her great advantages of soil and climate, far in the rear of States born but yesterday. But for intelligence mingling with and directing labor, the world would yet be in its barbarous and savage infancy, and there would be no Gladstone to depict its youth, and the United States, instead of being peopled by sixty millions of the happiest human beings, would yet be the heritage of cruel tribes numbering less perhaps than the population of our chiefest city.

Education and intelligence do not always go hand in hand in the individual, but education is the parent of intelligence as intelligence is the parent of prosperity.

CHAPTER VI.

Prosperity in Proportion to Intelligence—Illiteracy in Southern, Western, and New England States—Ignorance is Poverty and Degradation for Whites and Blacks Alike—Poverty will Continue as long as Ignorance—Prosperity of the South Bound up with Elevation of the Laboring Population.

All then being agreed that intelligent labor is the basis of prosperity, may it not be fairly claimed that if a country otherwise favorably situated is not prosperous, it must be because its labor is not intelligent—and by labor is meant not merely those who drive the plow and swing the scythe, who handle the saw and push the plane, who ply the trowel and wield the hammer, but all who guide, plan and command—in a word, all who aid by hand or head in the production of wealth? And not only will all agree that intelligence is the parent of prosperity, but all will likewise agree that negro labor, which is our principal dependence, is extremely deficient both in education and intelligence. But while all may not agree that the white labor of the South is greatly lacking in intelligence and efficiency, yet those who are acquainted with white labor in the South and elsewhere will agree that even our white labor is inferior to similar labor elsewhere. The simple fact that (census 1880) 3,254,106 persons out of a total of 8,827,676 of the age of ten and upwards could not read, is strong evidence of lack of general intelligence. While in the eight Western States, from Michigan to Kansas, the proportion of illiterates is 413,547 to 10,785,090, in the six New England States it is 157,233 to 3,219,856, and in the three Middle States it is 351,899 to 8,050,634. This exhibit of itself may very well explain the great difference in prosperity and progress between South and North; and who can question that the South would be infinitely greater, wealthier and happier if her people were educated to the same extent as are the people North and West.

If, as heretofore claimed, there are causes for the absence of prosperity in the South, as already partially set forth, may not the principal cause be attributed to the lack of education and consequent inefficiency and degradation of our laboring population? That lack of education to the extent we see prevalent in the South, is the parent of inefficiency and degradation, is a proposition needing no demonstration, for education means brightening and sharpening man's mental faculties, purifying his morals and manners, and refining his tastes. The individual devoid of education is little above the plane of the brutes, and in some respects he is worse; for he has vices and passions the brute is a stranger to, and he exercises little or no restraint in their indulgence. Such a person is satisfied with life in its lowest phases, and as long as he has enough, regardless of kind or quality, to fill the belly, he has little or no desire to improve his degraded lot. This applies to whites as well as to blacks, for even under the shadow of our boasted seats of learning at Charlottesville and Lexington, the whites of the neighboring mountains are noted for their ignorance, indigence and degradation, and the same conditions exist in the mountain regions extending from Virginia to the plains of Georgia.

If, then, we may fairly attribute our lack of prosperity to the ignorance and degradation of our laboring population, does it not naturally and inevitably follow that our poverty will continue as long as the ignorance continues, and does it not equally follow that our expectation of prosperity will be a delusion until we elevate this population? And does it not further follow that as cause always acts logically we cannot elevate unless we take the logical and necessary steps leading to that end? Nature demands an equivalent always, and in enforcing her requirements she understands what Shylock, sharp Jew as he was, never learned—viz: how to get her pound of flesh without one drop of blood. However disagreeable, painful, and even repugnant things may be to us, they are all equally agreeable to nature, and when nature prescribes any medicine or course, however nauseous it may be, we must follow it or ignominiously fail. Nature requires that if we want bread we must not sow wheat in May, or if we want cotton we must not plant it in August; we may do it, but if we do nature says: Be ye hungry and be ye naked. Nature never allows us to gather figs when we have sowed thistles, nor grapes when we have planted thorns; nor, on the other hand, does she compel us to a diet of thorns and thistles when we have dliligently set out orchards and planted vineyards.

Thus our prosperity is bound up in the elevation of our laboring population; and we desire prosperity. Nature says to us, you are welcome to prosperity, just as much so as if you lived in New York, Massachusetts, or Ohio; but you must pay the price thereof, just as these States have done, and just as every other community must do. There are no dead heads with me. The South replies: Yes, we want prosperity, but we want it by letting our laboring population remain pretty much as they are. Nature responds: No, that won't answer; you are not even paying a penny for an immense good; you must pay the full price, which is the elevation of the people who do your work. We can't dodge the question, and we can't fool nature. We must follow her full prescription. We may, indeed, throw the medicine into the bucket, but if we do we still remain invalids.

Now as we go along we will endeavor to point out

clearly what must be done to elevate our laboring population. Some of the steps we have already taken—some in full, some only partially—but we are still proceeding in the right way. Other steps we will take after reflection and a little time given; other steps, again, will require a pretty strong effort, but they, too, will be taken; but some we—that is, the older generations—will positively refuse to take, and will vehemently swear not only that we cannot, but by the Eternal, as Old Hickory used to say, we will not take them.

As we go along we will point out the various steps thought necessary, and we hope that careful attention will be given, and that we may candidly weigh all that is said, for if we do not we might in our wilfulness overlook, or, because they are nauseous, deliberately refuse to take one or more essential steps, and thus render vain all our other efforts. If what is said be not of truth and wisdom, it will come to naught, and the writer will be the only sufferer, or, in the language of a higher authority: "For if this counsel or this work be of men, it will come to naught, but if it be of God, ye cannot overthrow it."

CHAPTER VII.

CAN THE NEGRO BE ELEVATED?

Examples of Progress Here—Field-Slaves Improvement on Relatives in Africa—House-Slaves an Improvement on Field-Slaves, and Freedmen Great Improvement on House-Slaves—Examples of Progress in Africa—Causes of Negro Degradation and of White Elevation—Status of the Negro in Europe and Brazil—Full Equality—Example of Society in Rio—Progress not Inalienable to Whites.

In treating of the elevation of our laboring population, I shall confine myself to the elevation of the negro, for though the elevation of our illiterate whites is also essential for our full prosperity, yet their elevation, as a matter of course, in a measure precedes that of the blacks.   The simple willingness of the whites to elevate the negro at once places them on a higher plane, and is a great step in advance for them, and as the additional necessary measures for the elevation of the negro are carried out, so their own elevation, proceeding from an enlightened and liberalized public sentiment, will also progress at a rapid rate.

It is a highly favorable augury of a bright future that, owing to a liberalized sentiment, the negro has in some parts of the South, notably in Virginia, been greatly improved, for a vast interval separates the negro of to-day from the negro of twenty years ago, and as the State has suffered no detriment from his elevation so far, it should be an encouragement for all good citizens to take the other necessary steps to bridge over the still vast chasm between what he now is, and what he must be, before he can become an enlightened and full-developed citizen; before he can become that efficient producer of wealth which is absolutely essential for our own prosperity.

But before treating of the elevation of the negro, let us first consider whether he is capable of elevation, for there is a wide-spread public sentiment, that he is capable of only a very moderate improvement—that as we have known him, so he must ever be; and if this opinion be true, then we had better at once shut up all his schools, and at once cease all efforts for his amelioration, for they must necessarily prove fruitless.

We will not, however, indulge in theory or quote stock sacred texts, showing the equality of all men, and therefore the equality of the negro, nor quote the assertion of evolutionists that all men have sprung from one human pair, but we will appeal to a few simple facts patent to all.

First, no one will deny that even our field hands were greatly superior to their relatives in Africa, and why? Simply because, our negroes had for many years been comfortably fed and clad, and the slaves had learned something from their white masters.

Second, no one will deny that house servants, especially those raised in the family, were greatly superior in appearance and every other respect to field hands, and why? Simply because their comforts had been much greater, and their associations had been more intimate with the better class of whites.

And third, when on Sundays, we enter negro churches and behold large, well dressed, and well behaved congregations presided over by pastors of good standing and ability; when we observe their numerous benevolent societies successfully conducted; when we enter their schools and see large numbers of obedient pupils, diligently studying their books, and when in their high schools we see exhibitions of scholarship creditable to the whites, with all their present and antecedent advantages, we must confess that here is an immense advance upon the house servant class. But although the interval between these last and the naked savages ranging African jungles and starving or subsisting mainly upon vermin is as great as from pole to pole, yet they are the same negroes which many of us claim are incapable of elevation, and all the difference between these antipodes is that our negroes have been exposed to many fostering surroundings. Now, nobody can deny that here is some elevation or improvement of our negroes, whether we call it ten, twenty or fifty per cent., and granting that the negro has advanced only ten per cent. under slightly favoring influences, who can deny the probability, nay, the certainty, of his advancing the whole scale of one hundred per cent. if exposed to the same favoring influences the whites have enjoyed for centuries; and as only good can come to the whites from the negro's elevation, we should honestly and even zealously take all the steps necessary to that end? The proposition that twice two is four, is very simple; but if we admit, also, that twice four is eight *because* twice two is four, we have a very small key, yet one that is sufficient for unlocking the most secret chambers of nature, and of explaining all the laws of the universe; so if we admit the simple proposition that our negroes have been elevated even slightly above their brethren, now dwelling in Africa, we furnish the believers in the complete elevation of the negro with a key that may, and that probably will, unloose all the formidable bars and bolts that at present obstruct his elevation.

But those who claim that the negro is incapable of material elevation point triumphantly to the fact that in the long course of history the negro has accomplished nothing in the line of civilization, and they argue that if in the long past he has developed very slightly, if at all, therefore he will accomplish as little, which is nothing, in the long future.

While granting, but with some reservations, however, the general fact of the negro's small advance, the THERE-

FORE, or the deduction, is demurred to, on the ground that it is a *non sequitur*. If the negro has shown NO capacity of development from the lowest stage in which any of the family is found, then the *therefore* is logical and indisputable; but if the negro has shown anywhere *any* development from his lowest stage of beastiality, then the *therefore* is not only illogical, but the simple fact of any improvement is an incontrovertible argument for further improvement; and *the* further improvement is an incontrovertible argument for further and still further improvement, until at last equality with the highest type of mankind is reached.

Let us inquire briefly into the facts. Does every tribe or people in its native home, Africa, exhibit one dead level of immovable and unredeemable barbarism? If they do, the question of the elevation of the negro is settled at the outset; but if they do not, the game is just begun. That they do not, but that some negroes show considerable advance, is proved from the following extract from Herbert Spencer, in his chapter on Idol Worship and Fetich Worship:

"We find it (Fitichism) rampant when there are fortified towns, well-organized governments, large standing armies, prisons, police and sumptuary laws, considerable division of labor, periodical markets, regular shops and all the appliances, showing some progress in civilization."

Also by same in Political Institutions (Chapter I):

"Take, again, an African society—Dahomey. We find there a finished system of classes, six in number; complex governmental arrangements, with officia's always in pairs; an army divided into battalions, having reviews and sham fights; prisons, police and sumptuary laws; an agriculture which uses manure and grows a score kind of plants; moated towns, bridges and roads with turnpikes."

Again, in chaper II., quoting Baker:

"Passing suddenly from the wildest savagedom to semi-civilization, we come to Unyoro, where they have developed administration sub governors, taxes, good clothing, art, agriculture, architecture."

Besides these, there are the Abyssinians, the Ashantees, and the Zulus—all peoples who have defied the power of Great Britain, and who have developed into strong and stable, though bloody and despotic, governments.   If circumstances in Africa itself have elevated some negro tribes into powerful kingdoms, the argument, instead of being that the negro is incapable of improvement, is that he is capable of elevation, and that this elevation is proportioned to and dependent upon favorable surroundings, acting continuously for long periods of time.

But lest the reader be wearied, let us conclude this point with a most inadequate summary in parallel columns of the surroundings of whites and blacks, and then let us wonder, if we can, that the two colors are now as we find them, or then question that if the surroundings had been reversed whether we would not now be found at the bottom and the blacks at the top of civilization.

NATURAL SURROUNDINGS.

WHITES.	BLACKS.
Temperate zone.	Torrid zone.
Stimulating climate.	Debilitating climate.
Man invigorated by climate; therefore,	Man overpowered and degraded by climate; therefore,
Bold, free, energetic, intelligent.	Timid, slavish, indolent, stupi¹.
Many navigable streams.	No navigable streams.
Coasts deeply indented with gulfs, bays, sounds, and, therefore,	One unbroken coast-line, 1 bays, gulfs, sounds, and, there fore,
People encouraged to industry and accumulating wealth.	People sluggish and slothful, no encouragement to labor and no accumulation of wealth.

ARTIFICIAL SURROUNDINGS.

Freedom of person.	Abject slavery of person.
Laboring for self.	Toiling for others.
Hope of reward and prospect of advancement.	Little hope of reward and no prospect of advancement.
Wealth, with its innumerable advantages.	Indigence, with its numberless drawbacks.
Fostering influences of every kind.	Debasing influences of every kind.
Weight of society light.	Weight of society crushing.

The Caucasian, but especially that branch of the family which dwells in the United States, like the Egyptians Assyrians, Persians, Greeks and Romans of the old world, and like the Chinese of both the ancient and modern world, for the Chinese whom we think unworthy to breathe the free air of heaven in our glorious country appear to have been a powerful empire long before the first stone of the pyramid of Cheops was laid, long before Helen was ravished from ante-classic Greece, and long before Lupa, untrue to her nature, nursed instead of devoured Romulus and Remus, fondly but falsely imagines that the Caucasian is the favored child of heaven, and that the Almighty himself has specially, particularly, and exclusively endowed it with all the powers and capacities of civilization. But the real fact is, our remote ancestors were as scurvy a lot as ever scourged the earth, and even our mediæval ancestors were a roving set of pirates and freebooters, whose lives were spent in ravishing and then murdering women, in slaying infants and old men, and in reducing to slavery all able-bodied men who escaped the edge of the sword; and the civilization of us, the descendants of these monsters, is solely owing to favoring and fostering influences, mainly those of commerce, operating through centuries of time.

We laugh at the Chinese for the vanity of claiming celestial origin for their kingdom and emperor, but our vanity is much greater. The Chinese draw the line at King and State, but we, more civilized, but less modest, draw the line of divine favor so deftly that it will embrace all whites of any and every degree, but at the same time exclude each and all of every other color.

But although nowhere in the United States, either North or South, does the negro enjoy all the rights of the white, yet when we cast our eyes beyond the limits of our country, the supposed home of the free, we find the negro occupying the status of *full* equality. In England and in

France, countries which have led in the race of civilization and of liberty, and which are still in the van of enlightenment, the negro rests under no political or social ban, but is received everywhere according to his merits and credentials, and if the negro has good letters of introduction he will be received everywhere, while the white man, if not so provided, will be totally ignored. And in the empire of Brazil, whose ruler has a world-wide reputation for goodness and wisdom, the negro is accorded full social and political equality. A Virginian, who was for eight years from 1853 United States consul at Rio, tells me that when he was there one of the emperor's ministers and one of the court physicians were black negroes; that he had danced with negroes at parties and official receptions, and that many of them, educated in Europe and favored with wealth, were much more elegantly cultured than he was himself.

And let not such who disbelieve the capacity of the negro for elevation imagine that perpetual progress is the inalienable inheritance of the Caucasian, who as implicitly believes that he is the favored child of heaven as do the almond-eyed Celestials, for the slightest acquaintance with history and with the career of individuals around them must convince them that a people grows in wealth and power as long as favoring influences predominate, and declines when adverse influences prevail. Greece, in her days of imperishable renown, and Greece in her abject humiliation under Turkish rule, is one of many striking illustrations of this truth as applied to nations, and we almost daily have equally striking illustrations as regards the individual when we see the individual and the family falling through poverty, vice or recklessness from the top to the bottom of society.

If there is any truth in experience, then experience teaches that the negro, degraded as we think him, and degraded as he really is, can be elevated when exposed to the same fostering influences that have surrounded us.

Chapter VIII.

Why not let Time Elevate?—Our Lives Too Short—Must Hasten and Assist Natural Process of Time—Elevation cannot be Summary; must have Cordial Co-operation of the Whites—Elevation of the Negro does not mean Negro Domination; Why?

Seeing now that the negro can be elevated—seeing that he has been elevated, elevation and degradation being simply the logical consequences of favorable or adverse agencies—what are we going to do? Shall we oppose or shall we drift and take chances of killing or curing, or shall we promote the negro's progress? Prejudice counsels the first, timidity the second, common sense the third; so what shall we do?

The majority will probably say, Wait; why take any steps to correct any abuses or to counteract any injurious consequences associated with his present degraded condition, for, say they, evils will in time cure themselves. But although history and observation abundantly prove that evils do not always work their own cure, but as often or oftener effect the ruin of the patient, we will admit that time will happily effect a solution of the negro problem; but then we must remember that time is not only a very uncertain, but also a very long something, and while we are waiting for this time we will be really suffering all the evils and disadvantages of actual poverty, which should not be thought of. In all other things we endeavor to abridge the natural process of time, and so should we in the gravest question before us—namely, the elevation of the negro.

If our lives lengthened into centuries, like those of the patriarchs, there might be little cause for haste, for one generation would have ample time to witness the perfection of this and of many other reforms; but when, in these degenerate days, man's span is shortened to a paltry three score years and ten, a generation, if things are left to drift, will pass away before it can see one single reform of importance accomplished. Thus, if we take no steps to hasten the negro's perfect enfranchisement and elevation, upon which our power and prosperity are dependent, not only this, but most probably other generations will disappear before we will escape from our present condition of poverty and ignorance, already partially set forth. Man's life is now too short to wait for the natural process of time, which may or may not work a cure, but he must hasten nature and take a hand himself, and he does, when wise, take a hand, and greatly to his advantage. If the elevation of the negro would not make us wealthy and prosperous, instead of advocating his cause, it would be the part of wisdom to promote any and all measures that would tend speedily to wipe him off the face of the earth; for to remain as he is, is not to be a citizen, but, in spite of the ballot, to be a serf; and to remain as he is, is to be a clog upon the South in her efforts to become wealthy, powerful, and respected by the other portions of the Union, and by the world at large. At present we are contemned by more than half the United States, and are totally ignored by the world.

The measures necessary for the elevation of the negro cannot be carried out summarily or by simple act of legislation, but they require time, care, wisdom and patience, and are impossible without the acquiescence and cordial co-operation of the whites. The negroes might be given the full benefit of their numbers, so that they absolutely controlled all the Southern States, either by numerical superiority or by combination with a minority of the whites, but, with the whites opposed, they could not hold power for any length of time, for the superior intellect and stronger will of the whites would soon, through intimidation or fraud, or by both, cow and scatter their leaders, when the negroes, being like sheep without shepherds, would, if the contest had been long and embittered, be in danger of actual bondage. Great as is the power of the National Government, it cannot elevate the negroes itself, nor can it force the whites to do so. The question is, we may say, absolutely within control of the whites. They can keep the negro in his present degraded condition, but they cannot do so without at the same time laying the axe at the root of their own welfare; and they can crush, but while doing this, they will be like Samson, who could only destroy his enemies by destroying himself.

The whites cannot see this now, for they are dominated by a great apprehension—namely, that the elevation of the negro means the degradation of the whites—and until this fear is allayed by showing them that little probable harm can accrue to them thereby, it will be like appealing to the winds to urge them to steps leading to the complete elevation and enfranchisement of the negro. In spite of all exhortation to love our neighbor as ourself, human nature will persist in loving itself better than its neighbor, and so, as long as the Southern people believe that the complete elevation of the negro will be an injury to them, they cannot be expected to take kindly, or even to take at all, to the idea. Show one that his interest lies in a certain direction, and there is little difficulty in getting him to go that way. Even religion is in vain unless it can show the sinner that it will confer an actual benefit upon him either here or elsewhere; and so to elevate the negro, we must show the whites that his elevation will be no detriment to them, and to prove this is the whole tenor and object of this essay.

There is, however, one error, or rather delusion, that we must guard against. To elevate the negro will, of course, greatly lessen the interval between the two colors; but because the gap will thereby be diminished, we must not jump at the illogical conclusion that the gap will be lessened by the debasement in any manner of the

whites. We unconsciously, but logically, reason to ourselves that to elevate partially necessarily means to elevate completely; that if we raise the negro even so little
as ten per cent. there is no logical stopping point short of
one hundred per cent.; that, therefore, in time the two
races will most probably meet on the same plane; but we
must not infer, for that would be an error, that this plane
will be reached by ascent of the negro and descent of the
white, both meeting on a common plane a little higher
than midway between the two. It is difficult not so to
conclude, because it is instinctive with us, but though
instinct may and does answer for brutes, it is a very poor
guide for human beings. There never was a greater
delusion than this instinctive apprehension of deteriora-
tion of the whites; for bad as human nature is, it does
not voluntarily desert the higher and the better for the
lower and the worse. As a localism here has it: You
can't fool one with corn bread when biscuits are on the
table. The colors will not meet half-way or anywhere
near it, but the smaller and weaker will gravitate to the
bigger and stronger, just as in the material world, and in
time the negro will probably rise to the plane of the white.
Blind and selfish human nature, which is honey-combed
with envy and jealousy, will object to seeing the negro
anything better than a despised and degraded creature,
speaking with bated breath and bowing with head uncov-
ered at its slightest nod, and such nature, already
degraded, will, of course, feel itself humiliated when it
loses its arbitrary hold upon its former dependents, but
enlightened human nature will not be and will not feel
itself degraded because the negro has been enabled
through merit to climb up to the higher plane, any more
than a gentleman will feel degraded because his carpenter,
butcher, shoemaker, or what not, builds a handsome home
next door; on the contrary, a gentleman will rejoice that
such a social inferior had by intelligence and industry
elevated himself in the social scale.

CHAPTER IX.

To Elevate must Inspire with Hope and Self-Respect—Negro has
  Little of Either—Caste—The South a Land of Caste and Privilege—All Whites in Highest, all Negroes in Lowest Caste.

Before we can make men of depraved and degraded
human beings, be they negro, semite, or even Caucasian,
and therefore efficient producers of wealth, there are three
principal things to be done. They must be inspired with
self-respect, their hope must be stimulated and their intelligence must be cultivated, and especially so with the
negro, for his self-respect is feeble, his hope faint, and his
intelligence slight; he must economically, morally, and
socially be born again, and self-respect, hope and intelligence are the trinity that will work out his elevation, and
they are also the rule of three to work out our own material regeneration.

Self-respect is, in general terms, that quality that
prevents our stealing, lying, drunkenness, idling, neglect-
ing family, &c., and the man that is materially lacking
in self-respect is generally little better than rotten drift-
wood, and incapable of accomplishing any good for the
society in which he lives. In passing, we mention that
two of our greatest men have been singular and contradictory examples of this influence of self-respect. Washington possessed it to such an abnormal degree he was
almost unapproachable, and Jupiter himself, in his
severest moods, was addressed by his inferior deities with
scarce more reverence than was Washington by his associ-
ates. On the other hand, General Grant at one period of his
early military life was so lacking in self-respect that his

fellow-officers obliged him to place his resignation in their hands to be held *in terrorem* over him, and yet they were finally obliged to forward it to headquarters. His subsequent career for many years was a painful exhibition of the effects of the lack of self-respect.

Hope is, in general terms, that sentiment that leads us to expect rewards from our exertions, and that stimulates us to effort. When hope is faint we can accomplish little, and when hope is extinct we slavishly submit to fate and sheepishly yield all that we have, even our lives, to the first comer. But where hope is strong, and where we can reasonably expect an adequate return for our labor, there we witness abounding prosperity, as in the commercial and manufacturing sections of our country, and, indeed, in all new countries; and where hope, even though dead, revives, we behold the same Grant emerge from poverty and degradation and become the greatest soldier of recent times.

Intelligence is, in general terms, that fruit of the training of the nervous system, of which the brain is merely the crown, which enables us to perceive objects and situations in their true light and relationship; which enables us to grasp and avail ourselves of attending circumstances that will assist us to accomplish our object with the least expenditure, and which enables us to perceive and to avoid those difficulties and impediments that will thwart us altogether, or that will cause us to expend unnecessary effort.

The negro is greatly deficient in all these cardinal qualifications. His self-respect is so small he pays little regard to chastity or the marriage vow, and bastardy is very general; he pays little regard to honesty, and when his necessities or his inclinations combine with opportunity, the difference between *meum et tuum* is reduced to its least expression; and he pays little regard for truth, for he looks upon lying and deceit as very venial faults, if indeed they be faults at all.

And what hope has the negro, and what stimulus does it exert upon him? Alas, in the present attitude of public sentiment he can have but little hope, and hope can supply him with small incentive. And why? because he is looked upon with contempt as a degraded inferior simply by virtue of having a black skin. A negro may be learned, pious or distinguished, he may have rendered great services to his country or to humanity, he may be honored in England, France and Germany, but when he comes among us who are so superior to the flower of Europe, he is at once sent to coventry. If he should obtain accommodation at hotels he receives them surreptitiously, and if any family, be it clerical, professional or mercantile, should receive him except as an inferior and as an act of condescension, as we sometimes invite inferiors to take a seat in our presence, that family is at once, or would be, put under the social ban. Not only if one is a negro, but if he has, or is even suspected to have, one drop of negro blood, he is placed under almost every disadvantage, and he can never feel safe from snubs, insults, or even kicks from the superior whites. In other words, the negro is the victim of caste.

In countries where caste prevails, there is little hope of progress for the inferior castes, and none at all for the lowest caste of all. In such countries, if people are born in a stable, they and their descendants are doomed to remain forever in a stable, and as they happen to be born in a higher station, there they remain perpetually. In India, *the* land of castes, the Brahmin is the highest caste; and whether rich or poor, whether a menial or a lordly idler, neither he nor his neighbors ever forget the fact; and such is the power, such is the influence, of caste that though he be cook to the viceroy from far distant Albion, he regards himself and is so considered by his fellows as superior even to the august and powerful Governor-Gen-

3

eral, who in great measure controls the destinies of his
millions of feeble and helpless brethren (252,541,210
census 1881).

The South, also, is a veritable land of caste, and its
chains hang heavily upon those of the lowest caste. In
the palmy days of slavery, when one man held in his
hand the lives of a thousand, there were several castes;
but now, though there are still many social and other
gradations, there are primarily only two castes.

Then there was first in rank and influence the caste of
educated and wealthy planters, who assumed the airs and
imitated the manners of the most exclusive aristocracy of
England and France, whence their families had immi-
grated. In Virginia, Louisiana and South Carolina, but
especially in the last State, many were highly cultivated
and intellectual, were polished and refined to a high
degree, the men being elegant and chivalric, and the
women charming and beautiful. In them we beheld all
that was noble and attractive in the system of caste.
Next came an intermediate caste of planters. They were
frequently men of wealth, but without education and of
little refinement, and though they met the first caste on
nearly equal but yet deferential terms on the hustings
and court green, the families of the two castes never
thought of visiting socially. Then came the overseer
caste. This caste, usually hard and heartless, was composed mainly of men who had been overseers, but who
had acquired a few slaves, and had set up for themselves.
Although the men mingled on semi-equal terms with
those next above them, they were generally looked down
upon, if not despised; and their families, as a rule, never
thought of visiting socially the families of those above them.
Finally came the "poor white" caste, possessed of no
negroes, but of a few acres, and despised alike by whites
and blacks.

The negroes, of course, were lower still, but they were

hardly considered as human beings. They were regarded
pretty much like horses and cattle, simply as instruments
like them, to enable the other castes to live, some in
elegance, some in ease, but all in comfort without thought
and without toil. They were treated, too, pretty much as
cattle; many, when the masters were kind, treated mildly
and their physical necessities carefully provided for; and
many, when the masters were harsh and brutal, treated
with cruelty and sometimes worked or beaten to death, it
being a maxim with some cotton planters that it was
cheaper to work a negro to death and buy another than
to work him reasonably and prolong his life.

But now, in the new order of things, all these castes
have become amalgamated into one, and a new caste has
been formed of those who were formerly considered too
low to form a caste at all, and Southern society is now
virtually divided into two castes. In the first caste are
merged indiscriminately gentleman, farmer, overseer, poor
white, and each and every one of these, regardless of
education, worth, refinement, decency or morality, belongs
to this class simply by reason of a white skin. The second caste is composed promiscuously of all who have a
black skin and all related to them, however remotely;
and all who are thus marked, however cultured and
refined they may be, however able and however excellent, are confined as by fate to this caste, and are not
permitted to throw off its galling chains; and society, by
its inexorable verdict, decrees that the meanest, lowest,
and most degraded of the first caste are, *ipso facto*, the
irreversible and perpetual superiors of the best, highest
and ablest of the second caste.

Hope cannot exist, certainly cannot flourish, under such
a weight. If he is to remain forever a "nigger," an
object of undisguised contempt, even to the lowest whites,
the negro will natually say to himself, Why strive, why
labor, why practice painful self-denial in order to rise, if

I am to derive no good from my effort? On the contrary, he will not exert himself, but will sink into despondency, and instead of becoming a net producer, and thus an instrument of our own prosperity, he will continue as he is, a depredator upon others' industry and a consumer of wealth. The South can never become prosperous, with its laboring population bereft of hope. Without hope the proudest Anglo-Saxon sinks into despair—much more the helpless negro, who is little more than a child.

Chapter X.

If Highest Caste will not Elevate must Crush Lowest Caste to Powder—Race Prejudice must be Mollified and Obliterated—Prejudice Mark of Inferiority—Courts of Justice must be Impartial to All Colors—Why Negroes do not Enjoy such Impartiality—Whites Kind to Negroes Individually, but Kindness must be Accepted as Inferiors.

If the negro is not to be elevated to the full standard, then clap on the shackles again and reduce him speedily to bondage when he can be made to work; no, not reduce him to slavery, because all history proves that slavery is finally destructive of the master caste, but put him between the upper and the nether millstone, turn on the water, and quickly grind him out of existence, for otherwise he must necessarily become a thorn in the side of society; for having once tasted the sweets of partial enfranchisement, he will not cease his efforts to obtain complete enfranchisement and equality until they are crowned with success, or until he is again reduced to abject submission. This period of trial or probation may continue for a few years, or it may be indefinitely, but whether it lasts for centuries or merely for years, it must be a period of anxiety and impoverishment for the whites. But the South *must* do something; it can't say I won't do anything, or I will fold my hands and see what will happen. The South, impelled by the current of events, has done a great deal, and it is still doing much, but a vast deal yet remains to be done, and the point is to prove to the South that it is its interest to do this great deal more, and to do it without unnecessary delay.

The first, the most important and the most difficult
step to take, is to mollify and finally to obliterate race and
color prejudice, a prejudice by no means peculiar to the
South or to white and black races, for until very recent
years the Frenchman had neither charity nor justice for
the Englishman, though separated only by a narrow strip
of water, and the Englishman reciprocated in kind and
with usurous interest, and although divided only by an
imaginary line, the prejudices between Englishman and
Scotchman were notorious; and even to-day the Englishman is ruled by prejudice when Ireland and her claims
are in question. But these race prejudices have now
measurably disappeared, and they will finally become
practically extinct as intercourse, commercial and otherwise, makes nations mutually acquainted. And not only
national, but personal prejudices of all kinds also disappear as intelligence is disseminated. Prejudice against
color itself has quite disappeared among Latin nations,
and is quite unknown in Great Britain, our worthy exem-
plar in so many respects, where a negro stands on his
merits like other people. But a general exclamation will
arise that prejudice against color is ineradicable, and that
we can never, never overcome it. Such a confession
involves two contradictory assertions, both of which are
equally erroneous. It implies that we are superior to the
great European nations, and in the same breath that we
are inferior to them—superior in that we are too wise to
follow their example and divest ourselves of prejudice
against color, and inferior in that we are unwilling or
unable to do so. Neither is true; and if European nations
have found it wise to break down the prejudice against
color it will not be wise, but foolish, for us not to follow
their example; and if they have been able and willing to
throw off the shackles of prejudice, we are dishonoring
ourselves to say or to think that we cannot do so likewise.
Many glory in prejudice, foolishly thinking it a mark of

superiority, but prejudice is always a weakness, and when it is extreme it is a badge of dishonor. The prejudiced are as they are because they do not see things in their true light, and are like a horse that shies and throws its rider to death because it sees in the simple clod, stone or stump a frightful spectre about to spring upon and devour him. The clearer one sees and the more enlightened he is, the freer he is from prejudice, which may be termed seeing things in a false light. And for so many generations past we have been looking upon the negro in a false light we cannot see him and his rights in their true light, and we shy violently and run the risk of wrecking our whole material welfare at the ideas of elevation, equality, manhood, &c., for the negro. Southerners cannot be true to their lofty character to be either unwilling or incapable of overcoming color prejudice, nor true to their interests either.

And while mollifying and finally correcting our prejudices, we must also modify our actions before we can inspire the negro with the self-respect and hope that are essential to making him a good citizen and an efficient producer of wealth. And the first duty resting upon us in this respect is to see that in criminal matters—that is to say, in matters of life and liberty—the scales of justice hang more level between whites and blacks; that the hand of justice bears more equally upon the two colors, and that both are punished alike for similar offenses, although it would seem reasonable to inflict heavier penalties upon the whites because they occupy a much higher plane morally, socially and intellectually, and are therefore less excusable for violating law; and we must see that our courts of justice, the most august and beneficent product of civilization, are an equal refuge for the wronged of all colors, and an equal terror to all wrong-doers, irrespective of previous condition.

And is not the law the same for all; and does it make any distinction between rich and poor, white and black?

 asdf asdf asdf asdfasfd asdf asdf

Literally, the law is the same for all. Then what more can be desired? The trouble is not that the laws are partial, though some of its enactments—namely, the whipping-post, chain-gang and poll tax laws—were aimed principally against the negro; but the trouble is with the interpretation of the laws by the juries, who merely voice public sentiment, which is superior to the law itself. The average jury is a whimsical creature, subject to all kinds of influences, though mostly of a sentimental character. In criminal matters, where whites are concerned, it seems ever to lean to the defense; and the strongest arguments of the prosecution are easily offset and upset by appeals on behalf of youth, family, station, respectability, &c.; or perhaps the whole family, weeping, is placed in full view of the jury; and the susceptible jury—sure at least in such cases to weep with them that weep—speedily brings in a verdict of acquittal where guilt is clearly manifest; or it says jail where it ought to say penitentiary; or one year where it ought to say ten, and ten years where it ought to pronounce death. But the negro has none of these sentimental advantages. Too poor to employ competent counsel, his liberty and life are necessarily committed to incompetent hands, when the proverb of poor pay poor preach becomes reality. But more unfortunate still, what sentiment can a poor ignorant, unkempt negro inspire, who thinks of his family, of his wife bowed down with grief, of his little ones deprived of a father's support and suffering for bread? The idea is preposterous, and so the jury, without difficulty, brings in its verdict of jail, penitentiary, or even death. The negro may be rightly punished, and he may receive no more than his just deserts, but if this is so, then the white receives less than his due deserts; or if the white is judged none too leniently, then the negro is judged altogether too harshly.

As long as the negro sees this state of affairs continue; as long as justice appears to him to slip aside her bandage when he is brought before her august tribunal, and judge him according to his previous and present condition, he must be bowed down with dread and humiliation, and whatever hope he may have nourished must die within him. But when he sees that similar offenses meet with equal punishments, irrespective of color or previous condition, then however severely he may be chastised, his self-respect and hope will not be offended; but on the contrary, they will spring up and strengthen, and make him a man—make him an efficient agent in promoting that prosperity of which we are ever dreaming but never beholding. In civil suits, where the judges, in Virginia, at least, practically, through their instructions, decide the case, the negro receives substantial justice.

But are negroes treated unfairly by juries and public opinion? Yes, and the experience and observation of every fair-minded man will confirm the assertion. One cardinal proof is that a white man seldom receives punishment for assault, however brutal, however unprovoked, however cowardly—be it maiming, homicide or murder upon a negro—unless, forsooth, the assailant be some degraded creature, disowned by his own caste. Of the numberless instances—running into the thousands during the past twenty-three years—of homicides, and murder of blacks by whites, there is no single instance of capital punishment, and few, very few, instances of imprisonment beyond a few months in jail, or a slight fine. The fact is the juries, which are the sole judges of the evidence, will accept testimony against a negro that they would reject in the case of whites ; and on the other hand they will frequently reject, or at least discredit, testimony of the negro against the white man, however well supported it may be. But to compound for sins we are inclined to by damning those we have no mind to, in case of any difficulty between white and black, and the former is injured or loses his life; lucky is the latter, if the homi-

cide is not declared by the crowd to be murder—when
courts of justice, though sure to inflict the highest penalty
in his case, are found to be too slow, and he is dragged
forth and slain, unshrived and unshriven, as if he were a
monstrous wild beast of whose presence earth could not be
rid too quickly.

As bearing on this point, the following is copied from
the Richmond *Dispatch* as I am writing this chapter.
Many other examples could be selected in the course of
any month. All these wretches were negroes, whom
justice, entirely untempered by mercy, would not have
suffered to escape, and there was therefore absolutely no
excuse and no necessity for these assassinations:

[Special telegram to the Dispatch.]

RALEIGH, N. C., September 14.—News was received here to-
night of another lynching, which is the *thirteenth* this year. It
occurred at Whiteville, Columbus county, night before last. A
body of masked men, a hundred or more, entered the jail and
demanded the keys from the jailer. With a score of revolvers
pointed at him he surrendered the keys, and the lynchers went to
the cell where Sherman Farrier (colored) was confined for an out-
rage committed on an aged white woman, took him and departed.
Yesterday, suspended to the limb of a large oak about one mile
from the jail, the body of Sherman Farrier was found with a
placard pinned on his breast bearing the words : " We protect the
virtue of our women. Beware." Farrier was a man of bad character, and had repeatedly been engaged in robbery. He was
given a preliminary hearing before two magistrates last Monday,
and was committed to jail to await trial. The evidence against
him was conclusive.

We will here mention a singular phase of Southern white
life, and that is, the slain or injured is *always* the guilty
party, and nowhere else in the wide world does justice
so accurately apportion penalty. The slain *must* be the
guilty party, for the white slayer of his white brother is
never punished, or hardly ever, and is almost always
acquitted with honor. Acquittal usually means innocence, but universal acquittal can only mean universal
innocence, and universal guilt of the maimed or slain.
As a matter of fact, it is safer in the South for a respect-

able white man to slay his neighbor than to kill his neighbor's dog; for killing the man rarely means more than a short time in jail, a feeble trial, and an acquittal with *eclat*, of course a round legal fee; but killing the dog means almost as generally an accounting with the owner of the dog, in which case the murderous revolver may take an active part.

But let it not be supposed from the foregoing that the whites individually are not just to the negro; they are much more considerate of his wants and feelings than are Northern people. But as a rule our kindness is bestowed as condescension, and it must be received with all due humility and with a tacit acknowledgment of inferiority of status; for let the negro betray even a moderate sense of equality or manhood, he is then thought "impudent," and our kindness takes affront. Until the negro sees and feels that the community fully recognizes that courts of justice are as much a refuge for him and as much a bulwark of his life and liberty as for the highest and the proudest, he can never feel sure of his position, and as long as what he enjoys is by favor or condescension, he can never be certain that what he enjoys to-day may not be arbitrarily wrested from him to-morrow, and until he sees that what he enjoys is by inalienable right, can he have that sense of security and manhood that are essential for an efficient wealth-producer.

CHAPTER XI.

OTHER THINGS WE MUST DO.

The Negroes should be Allowed Free Admission to All Hotels, Theatres, Churches, and Official Receptions—Such Places not Private Property—Why they Belong to the Whole Public—Why Negroes should not be Restricted to Places for Negroes—If so, Same Principle of Segregation should be Applied to Other Things and to People of Each State—Example of Drummer—Imaginary Examples, &c.

The negro must be allowed free access to all hotels and other places of public entertainment; he must be allowed free admittance to all theatres and other places of public amusement; he must be allowed free entrance to all churches, and in all public and official receptions of president, governor, mayor, &c. he must not be excluded by a hostile caste sentiment. In all these things and in all these places he must, unless we wish to clip his hope and crush his self-respect, be treated precisely like the whites, no better, but no worse.

In the capital of our great country, the respectable negro, though not welcomed, is admitted to the best hotels, to the best seats in theatres, to the best churches, and in presidential receptions he meets with no humiliating discriminations; yet when we come South as far as Richmond, only about 100 miles from Washington, we seem to be in a different country, we seem to be translated from a world of equality where worth makes the man to a land of caste where birth makes him. In

Richmond a riot is threatened when it is thought that a negro member of a Brooklyn white lodge intends occupying in company with his white brother, a first-class seat in the theatre. The hotels, except under extraordinary pressure, drive negroes from their doors; the leading congregations, except the Catholic, would go into a spasm and perhaps leave the house, were the negro to seat himself with the body of meek and lowly worshipers; and if a negro with his wife or sweetheart were to attend the governor's public reception, they would in a few minutes be the only guests, or they would be frozen, if not driven out. But perhaps we should not be surprised that such slight change of latitude should work such great difference, seeing that a slight variation at the creation produced all the vast difference between man and woman.

Let us put ourselves in the negro's place. Let us feel when passing good hotels there is no admission here; we dare not go in lest we be kicked out; when entering a theatre to be told to go up in the top gallery, no seat for you in the parquette; when entering an imposing church to be told rudely no place in God's house for you, unless there be a gallery, to which you are sent with indifference, or when seeking to attend an official reception, *your* governor's for instance, to be told brusquely no admittance; and suppose this treatment is continued year after year, and as far as we can see is likely to continue *ad infinitum*, would not we have our pride cut to the quick, and would not our *morale* be greatly lowered, and would we not be greatly handicapped in all our efforts to get along? There can be no doubt of it; and can we expect the ignorant, degraded, poverty-ridden negro to rise with such burdens resting upon him, and if he sees no prospect of the burdens lifting? Hope herself will not be able to stimulate him to exertion. We must lift these heavy burdens and grievous to be borne, and unless we do we can never have the negroes as co-workers in the production of wealth, and without their co-operation it will be vain to expect prosperity. We may continue to crush, and we may delight in the exhibition of our arbitrary power, but every oppression and every denial of the equal rights of the negroes will be at our own expense.

Many will excuse and defend this treatment of the negro on the ground that theatres, hotels and churches, are private property, and that to compel them to receive negroes on equal terms with whites would be to correct one wrong, if it be a wrong to treat them thus, by committing another. But although theatres, hotels and churches may be private property, they are public as regards their creation and their functions, and they are of the nature of railways which may be private property, but which are public institutions. As a railroad cannot build a track or run a car except by virtue of permission, called a charter, granted by the public, so no theatre can raise its curtain and no hotel can spread its table without the same permission, called a license, from the public, which means not some, but all the people, not whites alone, but whites and blacks. And churches are likewise public, because the community, which means all the people, exempts them from all taxation, and churches can become strictly private only by renouncing their public exemptions, and then they may impose any restrictions they choose upon would-be worshipers.

All these institutions are public—they belong to the public, and are for the public convenience—and they can as properly refuse accommodation to all whose noses indicate a semitic origin, all whose names or "rich brogue" betray Hibernian descent, or all whose "sweet accent" a la General Scott reveals Teutonic birth, as to refuse similar accommodation to all whose faces are black.

For public sentiment to shut the doors of any of these places in the faces of any portion of the community, is to degrade and to humiliate it, and is greatly to impair its ab....y to serve the best interests of society. But granting these institutions to be private property, their owners would not be injured when all were obliged to furnish similar accommodations to all classes, for in that case, caste purists would then have no occasion to desert one place for another, for they would be liable to meet everywhere the despised black face. Would I like being thrown at the same hotels and other places with negroes? No, but it would be very much easier to bear the shock to taste or fancy than to endure the shock to justice by depriving any fellow-creatures of their rights.

But others say let the negroes stick to their own hotels, their own places of public amusement, and their own churches. As a rule they will do so, for like prefers like the world over. But suppose some negroes on account of convenience, comfort or profit desire to go elsewhere, what then? Shall we say no, and in case of refusal shall we call in the police, and in a place like New York herd them together in Thompson street and other local ghetto?

This course would present a pretty state of affairs. Policemen would increase prodigiously in number, and blue cloth and brass buttons would rise to a monstrous price, for constables would be required at all the approaches to every city and town where negroes would likely travel in order to direct them to their appropriate places. In small cities this would not be very difficult, but in New York where distances are very great, the policemen, instead of guarding the city, would be employed in guiding the colored traveller, or, as many travellers would certainly prove refractory, would be engaged in dragging them to station-houses, which would then be so full of prisoners whose only crime was a matter of taste, that there would be no room for actual criminals. Cities, too, would be obliged sometimes to increase their debts on account of damages for false imprisonment, for dark brunettes are so much like mulattoes, mistakes are sure frequently to occur, like the following:

Some years ago a drummer, since become partner in his house, from my city, was urging an irascible North Carolina merchant to purchase his wares. He was, however, a little too persistent, and vexed the merchant, who cried out to him, "you damned yaller rascal, if you don't get out of here I'll kick you out." Before adopting the plan of segregration, our dark skinned Southern brethren should carefully reflect, for they might be corraled and introduced to the charms of Thompson street.

If the system of segregation were adopted for the blacks it would be well to extend its benefits to the people of all this glorious Union. There are thirty-eight States, all of whose citizens have more or less peculiarities, some of which are very offensive to the citizens of other States. Now, for the peace, comfort and quiet of the citizen, great cities like New York and Chicago should be divided into thirty-eight sections, properly marked, branded or painted—painting would be the most effective and picturesque, so that no town need ever be painted an uniform red—and when a train or boat arrived, the hackmen should not cry our Astor House, Fifth-avenue Hotel, &c., but the travellers should sing out Georgia, Ohio, New York, Massachusetts, &c., &c., when they would be taken in charge by the custodians of the various sections and properly directed. Then nobody would be shocked by color, whiskey, tobacco juice, profanity or any other habit, practice or forms of speech they were not accustomed to at home. Obviously, a modification of the plan would have to be made in small places like Richmond, and in the Southern cities. These cities cannot afford many hotels, and as visitors cannot be segregated, Yankees, Hoosiers, Wolverines, &c., should be refused admittance to any Southern hotel, because in the first place, they are not fit to associate even in hotels with high-toned Southerners; in the second place, because their "guessing," "had'nt ought tos," "do tells," &c., would clash painfully with our "few molasses," "hav'nt saws," "we–uns," "you–uns," &c., and because in the third place, their criticisms, verbal or by looks, of our favorite pastime of medallioning our floors with tobacco juice would be extremely disagreeable, and while excluding color because disagreeable or offensive, it would be well to exclude at the same time everything else distasteful, so that our hotel life may realize the ideal of perfect social intercourse. But what shall we do with visitors from Northern and Western States, whom the frantic efforts of our immigration societies induce to come South? That is easy enough. Partition off in the suburbs camping grounds or caravansereys for the various Northern and Western States, and tell them to bring their tents and "vittles" along. This would be a very nice arrangement, and the novelty of it would undoubtedly attract strangers from all parts of the world. Segregation is indeed an excellent plan, and the more excellent the more general should its benefits be diffused.

Chapter XII.

Negro Votes Freely in Virginia, North Carolina, and Tennessee, but not in the Six Southern States ; Why?—Tables Showing Population, Voting, State and Congressional Representation in Three Southern and Six other Southern States—Similar Tables for New York and Massachusetts and for Ohio and Illinois—Bad Effects of Not Voting—All should be Encouraged to Vote—Examples—Ballot to Virginia Negro Stands for Everything Great, Good and Glorious—Cultivation of Tobacco makes Virginia Negro Eager to Vote—Cultivation of Cotton makes South Carolina and Georgia Negro Apathetic—Religion may make South Carolina and Georgia Negro Indifferent to Ballot—Example of what South Carolina and Georgia Negro Yields for sake of Religion—Negroes of the Six Southern States only Apostolic Christians.

There is another right the negro does not fully enjoy in all parts of the South: this is the right preservative of all rights—

THE RIGHT OF THE BALLOT.

In Virginia, North Carolina and Tennessee, the negro, led by able and strong white minorities, exercises this right freely, and as few frauds are perpetrated to his injury as the two parties North and West practice against each other. But from South Carolina to Texas, the negro appears to have been as completely deprived of his electoral rights as have the whites been deprived of his servile labor.

The following tables would seem to prove this. The first table is of the three States where the negro enjoys his electoral rights; the second one is of the other six

Southern States east of the Mississippi, where it is believed the negro is deprived of his vote:

STATES.	Males Twenty-one and Upwards. Census 1880.		Congressional Election. 1886.		Legislature. 1887-'8.		Congr'ss 1888-'9.	
	White.	Black.	White Vote.	Rep. Vote.	White.	Republican.	Democratic.	Republican.
Virginia	206,248	128,257	102,221	123,080	100	40	4	6
North Carolina	189,732	105,018	114,811	82,393	98	72	7	2
Tennessee	250,055	80,250	125,157	105,856	81	48	8	2
Total	646,035	313,525	342,489	311,329	282	160	19	10
South Carolina	86,900	118,889	39,072	5,960	153	6	7	..
Georgia	177,967	143,471	25,398	1,895	189	30	10	..
Florida	34,210	27,489	83,385	23,152	79	18	2	..
Alabama	141,461	118,423	62,181	21,436	115	18	8	.
Louisiana	108,810	107,977	63,097	21,450	118	16	6	..
Mississippi	108,254	130,278	34,730	10,624	*130	19	6	..
Total	657,602	646,527	257,863	87,517	784	107	39	..

* Legislature 1884-'5.

We also present a similar table for two Northern and two Western States, the wealthiest, most intelligent and most influential of their respective sections. State elections are given because Democrat and Republican, owing to many side parties, do not show total votes:

STATES.	Males Twenty-one and Upwards. Census 1880.		State Election. 1886.	Legislature. 1886-'7.		Congr'ss 1888-'9.	
	Population.		Total Votes.	Democratic.	Republican.	Democratic.	Republican.
New York	1,108,571		976,371	66	91	51	19
Massachusetts	502,618		243,769	93	182	4	8
Ohio	826,577		701,429	58	89	6	15
Illinois	796,827		570,163	87	106	6	14
Total	3,534,623		2,485,732	301	471	31	56

We make a comparison below between the three groups as follows:

Males Twenty one and Upwards. Census 1880.		Percentage of Votes. 1886.		Legislature. 1887-'8.		Congr'ss 1888-'9.	
STATES.							
	White.	Black.	Whites.	Opposition.	Democratic.	Republican.	Democratic.	Republican.
Three Southern States .	646,035	313,525	53	100	282	160	19	10
Six Southern States .	657,602	646,527	39	13	784	107	39	..
Four N. and Western States. .	3,531,623		70		304	471	31	56

These are suggestive and instructive tables. Leaving out of view altogether the question of intimidation, and granting that there is none, the question is very pertinent whether public affairs are or can be in a healthy or flourishing condition when citizens take so little interest in politics that only thirty-nine per cent. of the whites and only thirteen per cent. of the blacks voted in the congressional election of 1886? When the citizen cares too little for public affairs to vote, experience proves that matters fall into a deep rut, that abuses multiply, and that government is conducted in the interest of political and corrupt rings, ruled by venal bosses. The South has abundant experience of this fact. The financial officers of Kentucky, Tennessee and Alabama were defaulters to large amounts, and in the financial department of Virginia one treasurer was convicted, though in a subsequent trial acquitted on the plea of insanity, of stealing, and two trusted clerks were sent to the penitentiary for robbing—one had continued his robberies for years and to a very large amount, for our treasury watch dogs had been narcotized by the uncontrolled sway of one party and were sound asleep. Uncontrolled party sway inducing indifference on the part of the voter begets favoritism and nepotism, public vices that Jefferson condemned by word and example. Thus in the Virginia capitol there were at one time five, perhaps more, of one family in office, only one of whom was well fitted for his place. They were father (clerk of the Legislature), brother (deputy), son (page), father who was about seventy-five years old when appointed, and brother-in-law (clerks in auditor's office). The auditor's office, the great financial heart of the State, was presided over by a gentleman whose ability never exceeded that of receiving teller of a bank, and the treasurer, an old gentleman when put in office, was elected by the Legislature on the petition of " had been " endorsed by "sentiment." Of the few deputies appointed by the auditor, one was the old gentleman aforesaid, the old gentleman's son-in-law, another old gentleman who was about seventy-five when appointed, and a clerk, who if not then a thief, was afterwards given full and unlimited authority to rob the State and spend the proceeds in luxurious living. When the healthy and vigorous action of the heart was so impeded and impaired, we can well imagine that the affairs of the State in its various members, the counties, were neither wisely nor faithfully managed. Matters had become so bad that a flood was required to wash them away. General Mahone saw and seized the opportunity, marshalled all the forces in opposition, and soon had almost as undisputed sway as his predecessors previously had. The rotten dead wood was swept aside, and although the new party had many sins, arising principally because its power was also absolute, to answer for, it cannot be fairly claimed that the new order of affairs was worse than the old. We then had so-called negro rule, but the Commonwealth survived, and, in the opinion of many, was much benefited.

Public affairs can prosper only when all the citizens are enough interested to vote. Compare the wealth, population and influence of Ohio with that of Georgia, already set forth, and see if there may not be some connection therewith in Ohio's vote in 1886 of 701,429 out of a *possible* vote of 826,577 in 1880, and Georgia's vote in 1886 of 27,293 out of a *possible* vote of 321,438 in 1880. The six Southern States instead of rejoicing, as they do, that they have their black fellow-citizens under absolute control, should stimulate all their citizens, white as well as black, for both need stimulation, to take an active and intelligent interest in public affairs, and to show that interest by voting. Competition is not only the life of trade, but competition of parties is the life of the Commonwealth. The only guarantee of continued good government in free countries is an active and intelligent interest in public affairs, and until that interest is excited and shown by a full and free vote public and private affairs are sure to languish. In Virginia, North Carolina and Tennessee the opposition votes freely, and in 1886 it cast its full strength; but these three States are inferior in no respect to the six other Southern States, but on the contrary are more prosperous and more influential in public affairs. Let the South revert to correct political principles, and she will not suffer, notwithstanding all the dire prophecies we hear from the ruling caste.

But, coming back to the question of intimidation, are the negroes intimidated and deprived of the ballot, or have they really lost their love of voting? We can not s v, but certain it is that something has changed their tastes in this respect.

There is said to be a great deal of human nature in the white man, and there probably is a great deal in the negro, too; but then, again, there may not be, and judging by the difference in his voting in the two groups of States, it is only fair to conclude either that there is very little human nature in some negroes, or that some negroes are not human beings. General Henry A. Wise, the distinguished father of the Hon. John S., was of the opinion that negroes were not human beings, but were Ebo Shins or Gizzard Foots; whatever they may be, though certainly things utterly beneath the regard of the noble Caucasian, and he was probably correct.

In Virginia the negro, or Ebo Shin, is infatuated with the ballot, and he seldom lets one pass without casting it. The ballot to him is the epitome of all that is good and noble. It stands in his eyes for deliverance from bondage; for wealth and honor; for public schools and churches; for military and benevolent societies—it stands in his eyes not only for everything he enjoys and hopes to enjoy, but for everything he has escaped. Thus looking upon the ballot, he prizes it above all his other earthly advantages, and when properly led and directed he would on no account forego the privilege of casting his vote. Crops suffering for work will not detain him from the polls, nor fatigue nor illness, unless actually confined to bed, nor even bribes; but, like a well-drilled phalanx, he marches up solidly, and votes solidly, too. Sometimes, of course, apathy overtakes the negroes as it does all other parties, and he may then be influenced by many reasons to remain away from the polls, or to vote with the whites; but let their leaders get them well in hand, and one had as well try to stop a stampede of soldiers or animals as to endeavor to keep them from voting their party ticket.

The ballot also means honor, for thereby he is raised from his low estate to proud positions of honor, and he becomes magistrate, assemblyman, congressman, one of the lawmakers of a great country. Aladdin's cave itself affords no more enchanting temptation than does the ballot offer to the Virginia negro. Yesterday a slave in chains, the ballot to-day seats him in the august halls of Congress. Fancy herself nowhere discloses a more striking transformation, and it is only comparable to nature when it unfolds the brilliant moth from the hideous grub.

The ballot also means emolument; no, not that, it means fabulous riches; for the negro who to-day may be sweating in the field for $8.00 a month, or at most $25.00 or $30.00 as porter, may to-morrow be given an office worth $1,000 or more a year, or he may be elected to the Legislature, where in one day he makes, without labor, almost the wages of a month, or he may be elected to Congress, where the fabulous sum of $5,000 a year and perquisites awaits him—and all by the grace of the ballot. A land flowing with milk and honey is nothing to these possibilities. It is like being beside the river Pactolus, where one has only to stretch out his hands and gather the golden sands. It is more to him than was Jerusalem to the Jew, or is mecca to the Mussulman, or is heaven to the Christian. Can we marvel, then, that the negro naturally values the ballot so highly?

In all this the negro betrays a great deal of human nature, and therefore one must say that the Virginia negro is a human being; but when we approach the South Carolina or Georgia negro we are completely mystified, and in spite of our love for all God's creatures, whether man, beast, or fish, we are not prepared to deny any charge that may be brought against the humanity of the negro of these States. Let us examine this species of negro. In hair, in color, and in other physical respects he is like the Virginia species, but when we investigate his mental characteristics the resemblance entirely ceases.

A thought here occurs. Science tells us that all nature is merely the creature of its constant surroundings. The Virginia negro makes tobacco, and has been making it for hundreds of years. The South Carolina and Georgia negro makes cotton, and has been making it for a century. Now can it be possible that the different environments of tobacco and cotton make all the vast difference that we observe between the two negroes? It is not only possible, but it *must* be the cause, and he is willfully blind or imbecile who does not see it.

The modern world contends that communities that vote are superior to those that do not vote. Communities being merely citizens in the aggregate, it follows that the Virginia negroes are superior to the negroes of South Carolina and Georgia, and it further follows that tobacco elevates and that cotton degrades. Thus it follows further, that those who denounce tobacco as the greatest evil except polygamy and whiskey, and those who forbid tobacco-loving preachers exhorting sinners to flee from the wrath to come, are altogether mistaken. The world must change its bearings and its attitude, and instead of anathematizing tobacco, it should preach a crusade in its favor, and should encourage its cultivation and its use, seeing what a great work it has wrought in the elevation of the Virginia negro. But we must compound for sins we are inclined to by damning those we have no mind to, and as the world must denounce something, let it denounce cotton and renounce its use, seeing the mischief it has wrought with the civic virtues of the South Carolina and Georgia negroes, who apparently have forgotten that they ever possessed such a thing as a ballot.

But if the tobacco and cotton theory does not satisfy, let us try the theory of religion. The negro is deeply emotional, and his thoughts dwell much in the spirit land. In his dreams, which are many, and which are not confined to the watches of the night, he, like Jacob, wrestles with the angel, and, like Jacob, he has a ladder resting on his prostrate body and extending into heaven, upon which angels ascend and descend and camp around him.

When walking through the dark shadows of the forest in the deep silence of night, he sees ghosts flitting now before and now behind him, and on his right hand and on

4

his left hand these spiritual beings accompany him.   He
lives in constant intercourse with the unseeable world and
his prayers are answered literally and speedily.   The
impenetrable veil that divides us from the so-called dade
is for him scarcely more than a veil of gauze through
which he sees easily, if not clearly.   He is a pilgrim and
a stranger here; his home is there—in the skies.   Here
all things are transitory and perishing; there all things
are permanent and immortal.   The illimitable future and
not the finite present, notwithstanding all its carnal
delights, which, however, he enjoys so meagerly, is the
reality to him.

Now is it not very probable that the South Carolina
and Georgia negro, having such views, cannot interest himself in such worldly matters as elections, and that he does
not vote, not because he is intimidated, but because of his
intense desire to win the spiritual race that is set before
him, and therefore he voluntarily lays aside every weight
that besets him, and he fears to vote, lest being embroiled
in the snares of political strife and ambition through
which he passed for a number of years, he may forget his
high calling and thus lose the crown.

The Virginia negroes, to whom we add the North Carolina and Tennessee negro, being the same species, having
been elevated, as we have seen, by the cultivation and use of
tobacco, prove their claims to humanity by entering boldly
the political arena and, though he numbers only half as
many as the whites, by securing for himself and friends
160 to 282 legislative seats and ten to nineteen congressional seats.   But the spiritualized South Carolina negro,
although he numbered in 1880, 118,889 to 86,900 whites,
both of voting age, tramples worldly honors and consid-
erations under foot, and reserves for himself and friends
only six out of 159 legislative seats, and he surrenders all
the congressional seats.   Five thousand dollars a year is
no temptation to him, but he prefers his humble cabin,

his plain and scanty fare and his small wages, provided
he may meekly cultivate the Christian graces and humbly
pursue the path to glory. If anybody's soul is to be lost
through the wicked wiles and temptations of Washington,
he is resolved it shall not be his soul, and he allows without a pang his white brother, who, however, repudiates
the relationship, to enjoy those great and worldly prizes.
The mighty Cincinnatus achieved imperishable renown
by preferring his plow to all the honors and rewards the
Mistress of the World could confer, but here is a stranger
sight still: thousands of unknown, unheard of, and unsung
black Cincinnati renouncing all that this world can confer in order to lead pious lives.

But some will say religion cannot be the cause, for if
so, why should the negroes of Virginia eagerly snatch all
the honors and rewards politics can give, while the
negroes of South Carolina despise them all? This is an
easy question. The difference is owing simply to the fact
that the spirit of Mahone operates in the first group of
States, and that the spirit of Sam Jones and Sam Small
operates in the other group.

Followers are necessarily like leaders, because leaders
are merely the exponent of prevailing sentiment.

Now Mahone, as is well known, is not only unorthodox,
but he is also extremely carnal, and seizes all the good
things of life without consulting conscience, eating what
is set before him without asking questions. He does not
ask questions on account of scruples but to save time;
for if it suited his purposes he would not only eat the
meat offered to idols, but also the idols themselves.

On the contrary, the two Sams are intensely spiritual.
They are forever hunting the devil; they spy him in
every bush, and when found they attack him so vehemently he ignominiously flies. Repent, renounce your
sins, seek the kingdom of heaven, is their constant
refrain; fly for your lives, the devil is right a̤ te̤r you, and

if you don't step right lively he has you sure, and then, oh, my soul, the rest is too frightful to contemplate. Sam Jones has evidently impressed his ideas indelibly upon *all* the people, for even the whites do not vote, only 25,398 having voted in Georgia in 1886, although fortunately they alone enjoy all the public offices. Mahone has demoralized all his negroes, and Sam Jones has spiritualized all his. Mahone's negroes are carnal, and therefore they clutch at everything within their reach; Sam Jones' negroes are thoroughly spiritualized, and they therefore take nothing within their grasp. The fact that the negroes of the six Southern States do not vote must be attributed solely to the disinterested effects of religion. It cannot be owing to intimidation, for the whites themselves scarcely vote, and who intimidates them?

By the way, nobody, we think, can fail from the foregoing exhibit to be convinced that the negroes of the six Southern States are the only true apostolic Christians now living. Holy Writ teaches us plainly that we cannot serve God and mammon. To white Christians this deliverance of divinity has little significance; for, while seeking the kingdom of Heaven, they never fail to hold on tightly to all the good things of this world, and instead of entering heaven by prayer, as the good hymn says, and with garments pure and white, they enter it, or think they do, with garments bespotted with grovelling tastes and passions, and with the rank odor of earth clinging to them as the smell of musk clings to the vulgarian using it. But to the South Carolina negroes this injunction is of living force, and, believing they cannot serve two masters, they yield allegiance unreservedly to the higher Master, Christ, and absolutely renounce the world. Thus did the Apostles.

Chapter XIII.

Why Negro Elevation does not mean Negro Rule—Total Change of Condition between 1865-78 and 1878-88—Statement of Changed Conditions—If a Free Vote means Negro Rule, then Negro Rule Prevails Over Eastern Virginia—Example of the Black Belt, or Fourth Congressional District in Virginia—A Free Ballot not Injurious to Virginia and Tennessee—Why Negroes are Inimical to Whites—Color Line the Work of Whites—Statesmanship Impossible while Color Line Continues.

But, laying aside badinage and irony, let us say without circumlocution, that the negroes of the six Southern States are intimidated and deprived of their ballots, for the whites not only acknowledge the fact, but plainly declare and believe that the negroes should be thus deprived in order to preserve stable and civilized government. If their fears are well grounded, then they are perfectly right in their course; for the first duty of man is to save the State, for a well governed State is the only soil in which permanent prosperity can flourish. The whites reason as follows: At the close of a four-years' war we found ourselves not only thoroughly exhausted, but also completely prostrate at the feet of our enemies. We found the negroes, everywhere numerous, but in many places and in some States in the majority, freed from slavery, and then made citizens; and we found that carpet-baggers and scalawags, by the aid of the negroes, naturally crazed with their freedom and its illimitable possibilities, got entire control of State, municipal and county affairs, and by frauds and robberies of every kind

made almost a complete wreck of organized society; and
because all these dreadful things happened when Federal
troops were everywhere, and when a simple lieutenant's
sword was weightier and mightier than the voice of any
community; when we were completely cowed, and did
not know how soon any of us might be arrested and
handed over to the military; when the negroes were
totally ignorant and necessarily intoxicated with their
freedom; when the passions of war were still active and
bitter, and when our conquerors were only too eager to find
cause of complaint against us; when the greed of carpet-
baggers and the greed and vindictiveness of scalawags
and refugee Unionists knew little or no restraint—because
such things happened in such a state of affairs, when
even worse things might have been apprehended, property and not life having been sacrificed, therefore similar
things will happen, when the whites are no longer inferiors, suspected and under martial law; when there are no
longer carpet-baggers and scalawags to lead the negroes
to their own ruin as well as that of the community; when
the negroes themselves have learned they can never rule
the whites, and when, above all, we have all the State
governments in our hands, and for years have had at
least one branch of the National Government to protect
us from unfriendly legislation. To argue thus is to be
absolutely illogical—is to be without even the shadow of a
foundation to rest upon. To take the ground that having
the power we intend to keep it, right or wrong, is easy of
comprehension, for we see that the law of the strongest
unfortunately still prevails too much everywhere, but for
reasonable men to argue that similar results will follow
almost totally dissimilar causes is indeed incomprehensi-
ble. If modern philosophy agrees on any one point it is
on this: that similar effects can result only from similar causes, acting in a similar way on similar objects;
change any single one of the conditions and the effects
are necessarily different.

Now, are not the conditions of the period from 1865 to the end of the Grant administration and of the period of 1876 to the present different almost as east is from west? And, being so different, how can any man who claims to be reasonable fear a return of the evil days of reconstruction by allowing the negroes their free right of voting?

Look at a few of the changed conditions:

THEN.	NOW.
Crushed, demoralized and disorganized.	Confident and disciplined.
Martial law.	Civil law.
Hostile administration and legislature.	Friendly administration and House.
Hostile judiciary and marshals.	Friendly judiciary and marshals.
Hostile State governments and legislatures.	State governments in our absolute control.
Negroes intoxicated with their freedom and unbounded in their anticipations.	Negroes sobered and humbled by experience—wiser.
Carpet-baggers and scalawags in full control.	Carpet-baggers and scalawags things of memory.

To perceive all these changed conditions and to be afraid of a return of former evil days is to prove that we are cowards, not Anglo-Saxons, or, if we are Anglo-Saxons, that we are not worthy of our ancestry; to perceive them and to be unwilling to restore the freedom of the ballot to the negro is to commit a crime against freedom; and not to see them when they are thrust before our eyes is to prove that we are blind, and that, like blind leaders, we will lead the State into a ditch.

To allow—yea, to encourage—the negroes to vote freely will not throw the State into the hands of the ignorant and corrupt, though the *personnel* of office-holders will be considerably changed. The most violent of the opponents of negro suffrage are and will be the office-holding and seeking class and their friends, who will cry, "Wolf!

wolf!" and who will frighten most the majority, composed of well-meaning but timid people.

But we are not left solely to reasoning in this matter, for, fortunately, we have experience to guide us. If the averment that freedom of the ballot for negroes means negro rule, then we have negro rule in the greater portion of Eastern Virginia. Ah! yes; and you are greatly surprised, are you not? For we have conjured up in our minds the idea that negro rule is some monstrous ogre that remorselessly devours everything that is good and desirable, and that scatters broadcast everything that is bad and baleful, and we cannot discover such a dreadful state of affairs anywhere near us.

But if freedom of ballot means, as is generally asserted, negro rule, then we must have negro rule in the greater portion of Eastern Virginia, because nobody claims that the negroes are intimidated or materially hindered from voting in Virginia, and nobody denies that the negroes vote solidly for their party. Therefore, if the negroes have the majority in any counties, and if they are not intimidated, and if they vote solidly for their party, then all counties with negro majorities must, as a rule, be under negro rule. Having a majority, not being intimidated from casting that majority, and actually casting that majority freely, there can be no possible escape from the actual fact of negro rule.

Now, are there any counties in Virginia where negroes are in the majority? Referring to United States census 1880 we find there are forty-two counties in Eastern Virginia, where the negroes are in an absolute majority, and where, being free to vote, there is consequently negro rule *in posse* if not *in esse.*

But let us take the example of the fourth congressional district, where the negro majorities are so large that negro rule exists not only *in posse*, but also *in esse.*

Thus:

Counties.	White.	Black.
Amelia	3,037	7,340
Brunswick	6,022	10,685
Dinwiddie	14,457	18,428
Greenesville	2,757	5,650
Lunenburg	4,611	6,924
Mecklenburg	8,222	16,388
Nottoway	3,012	8,144
Powhatan	2,726	5,091
Prince Edward	4,754	9,914
Prince George	3,255	6,799
Sussex	3,361	6,701
Total	56,214	102,064

Now, nobody can dispute that if the negroes are not intimidated, that if they vote freely, and that if, generally, they vote in a solid body, that here must be negro rule; or, if they deny negro rule here, where else in the South can they possibly fear negro rule? If nearly two negroes to one white does not, with a free ballot, constitute negro rule, then ten negroes to one white does not mean negro·rule; or if negro rule is escaped where this proportion of the colors exists, then negro rule will be escaped anywhere and everywhere in the South. Or if negro rule does not mean destructive government, where is the sense of representing negro rule as a return to reconstruction days, where not government but almost anarchy reigned?

If negro rule means all, or nearly all, the economic, political and social ills, or even partially, that the opponents of negro suffrage delight so much in picturing, then this fourth congressional district must be in a most lamentable condition—must be a cancerous spot on the fair form of Virginia that saps her whole prosperity. The fourth district may be in this condition, but before deciding let us compare it with the ninth congressional district, a strictly white as the fourth is a strictly black district, which contains per census of 1888: Whites, 133,055; blacks, 17,549. Total, 160,604. And with some facts contained in report of auditor of public accounts for the year ending September 30, 1886. The population of the two districts is very nearly the same. Negro rule being the logical and necessary result of unrestricted suffrage, we, of course, find in this fourth district material ruin and moral degradation, and the annual report of the financial officer of the State must show both conditions to prevail, or, if it does not, then the report must be of no value, or those who talk so glibly and so mournfully about negro rule are false guides and erring prophets.

If the fourth district is ruined financially it can pay no taxes, but the auditor either falsifies the returns or the two districts pay into the State treasury as follows:

	For State.	For Schools.	Total.
Fourth District—Black . . .	$74,988	55,770	$130,758
Ninth District—Whites . . .	65,609	50,862	116,471

So, then, it would appear that negro rule, which is synonymous with unrestricted suffrage, does not ruin to such an extent that it cannot contribute its fair share to public burdens and to public schools.

But, then, negro rule or unrestricted suffrage means official robbery and general demoralization, and perhaps this is the state of affairs in the fourth district, and, if so, the criminal charges ought to be very large. The auditor of the State reports in Table No. 19 the amounts he paid out for such expenses in 1886, and the following comparison is made: Fourth district, $22,173; ninth district, $33,376.

So, then, it would seem that an unrestricted vote and a fair count—or, in other words, negro rule—renders the fourth district not much worse off either financially or morally than the ninth district, where the negroes are few; and although of late years we hear of little else than of the great boom in Southwest Virginia, it must be confessed that if the figures of our auditor are correct the fourth district is as happy, moral and well off as the great ninth district.

Those who go around wearing the frightful scare-face of negro rule are doubtless honest in their apprehensions, but they are nevertheless doing an untold amount of evil to the South, which they love well but not wisely.

The fear of negro rule in the sense of the alarmists is a wild and pernicious chimera, and the experience in the fourth district ought to convince any honest man that it is. The negro appears to have no ambition to rule, for when he has the majority his almost invariable practice is to give the offices to the most capable white men in his party, and when he cannot get good men from his own ranks he selects worthy Democrats, and remains contented with the crumbs that fall from the official table or with the bones and fragments his white leaders throw him.

The six Southern States have no more to fear from a free and fair ballot than has the Fourth Virginia District, and if they are wise they will not only permit, but they will encourage, the negroes to vote; for it is only by inspiring all the people with interest in public affairs that they can expect prosperity. The three States of Virginia, North Carolina and Tennessee, where the opposition cast its full vote in 1886, are no less prosperous than are the six Southern States where the opposition cast only thirteen per cent. of its vote in 1886; but, on the contrary, they exhibit greater progress and prosperity, and certainly as much moral and intellectual development.

The negroes are against us simply because we treat them not as citizens, but as creatures who have no rights we are bound to respect. But let us respect their rights, and they will gladly coöperate with us. But as long as public affairs are conducted on the color line, which is in reality simply an appeal to passion, prejudice and selfish interests of the lowest kind, the negroes will remain solid. Wisdom and statesmanship can then have little voice in their management, for the color line deliberately banishes them from the council chamber and the legislature alike.

CHAPTER XIV.

Negro not a Competent Voter ; neither are Millions of White
Voters ; but Ballot Absolutely Essential to his Freedom—
Ruin of the Commonwealth that Degrades its Citizens—Tyranny Destroys the State and Demoralizes the Citizens—Southerners cannot Escape the Demoralizing Effects of Tyranny.

But the negro is not a competent voter, and he should
never have been entrusted with the ballot. That he is
not an intelligent voter in the sense of foreseeing the
necessity of wise laws, or of perceiving their bearings on
all points, is readily admitted ; but, then, who among our
millions of white voters, when tested by this standard,
are competent? Very few, indeed ; and very few of the
legislators and congressmen to whom we depute the
making of our laws are. But that the negro, as long as
he was not to be a slave, should have the ballot was
a matter of absolute necessity ; for if he had no ballot to
protect his newly acquired freedom, how long could he
keep it in the midst of powerful enemies, who regarded
him with bitter hostility, because, though once practically supreme master of his time, limb and life, they
could not then command his simplest movements? The
negroes would in that case have been literally sheep with
wolves for their shepherds. The ballot was, and is, as
absolutely essential for freedom as is the atmosphere for
life ; but let us not fondly imagine that while rendering
or seeking to render this right nugatory, and while consequently degrading the negroes, we are not injuring
ourselves.

It is doubtless very gratifying to our baser nature to

control absolutely the actions of a whole class of our fellow-creatures; but the enjoyment is suicidal, and it will end in our moral enfeeblement and in our material impoverishment, for ruin must follow communities that persistently degrade any large portion of its citizens. Tyranny, whether national or individual, degrades not only those imposed upon, but it also demoralizes the doers of the wrong, for nobody can deliberately wrong another without feeling humiliated himself, although the constant perpetration of injustice soon renders one callous to the sense of right and wrong. History represents both Nero and Prince Hal as promising youths; but after a while the practice of injustice so changed these fair young men they became monsters of iniquity and by-words of depravity; and so, in a measure, Southerners cannot escape a certain mental and moral obliquity, a certain lowering of the sense of right and wrong, by continuing deliberately to deprive their negro fellow-citizens of the greatest and most valuable of all their rights— namely, the right of suffrage; and when the moral tone is lowered all their undertakings must necessarily be injuriously affected thereby.

History is one long record of the fact that privilege, whether founded on brute force and stamped only on the fickle mind of the unbridled savage or cruel despot, or whether deeply imprinted on the social mind in the guise of unyielding caste, or whether crystallized in deliberate laws upon the statute book, has this dual effect of degrading and debasing the lower and of demoralizing and finally of debasing the higher, the grand finale being the stagnation or destruction of the State; and can the South expect to escape such consequences if it persists in maintaining its practical oligarchy (all oligarchies have been short-lived), whereby, though all are alike in the contemplation of law, at least half of the population of six States is practically deprived of the

most sacred right of freemen—the right freely to declare
its voice at the polls.

If the South desires prosperity it must, granting that
the negroes are not intimidated, encourage them to take
interest in public affairs, and to show their interest by
voting; and granting that the negroes are intimidated, it
is our double duty to put a stop to the suicidal practice,
for in these days of active competition the South needs
the active and intelligent coöperation of all its citizens in
order to prosper, but if by intimidation we cripple the
hopes and ambition of half the people who are our principal dependence for labor, we have nothing to hope for
but disaster. As well hamstring a horse or mule and
expect work from it as to expect valuable results from
degraded and hopeless labor.

But the negro has all his rights—let him use them.
Yes, he has them nominally, but the principal one, the
ballot, is held pretty much on the following tenure:

An officer on one occasion called for volunteers from
his assembled command for some desperate work. He
invited all who were unwilling to volunteer to step to the
front, but he added, with a Sheridan oath, that he would
shoot the first man that did so. If one is to be slain for
not volunteering, he prefers to go along and take chances;
and so the negro thinks that if he is to be intimidated
and even killed for exercising his nominal rights, he had
better forego them altogether.

The South will look in vain for prosperity as long as it
abridges the right of voting of any class of its citizens.

CHAPTER XV.

EDUCATION.

Its Vast Importance—Sums Spent Annually by Ohio, Michigan,
Indiana, and Illinois—Tables of Non-Readers and Non-
Writers in Eleven Southern States—Of the Press South and
other States—Of Higher Education—Many Lawyers, but Few
Mechanical, Scientific, or Literary Men in Southern States.

We have now come to the subject of education which,
from its great importance, we must treat at some length.

In these modern days, while there are many different
ideas as to methods of education, there are no two opinions as to the value and importance—nay, as to the necessity of education itself, and so strongly is this necessity felt
in many parts of the Union, for instance, in the central
States of Ohio, Michigan, Indiana and Illinois, they
spend vast sums annually for educational purposes, aver-
aging, according to the United States Bureau of Education, very nearly $30,000,000, which is an average of $10
for each of their children between seven and nineteen
years of age, or about $20 for each child actually attend-
ing school.

As education is the great lever that moves the world, it
is of vital importance to the prosperity and influence of
any country that this lever should be in good condition;
for now, if ever, knowledge is power and wealth too, and
education is the parent of knowledge. The South is no
exception to this general law; she holds no dispensation
whereby ignorance may do the work of knowledge, and if
she desires prosperity and influence, she, too, like the rest
of the world, must encourage education. Let us now see
what is the condition of education within her bounds.

We will first take the children of ten years of age and upwards, and divide them into readers and non-readers:

STATES.	Census of 1880. Ten Years and Upwards. Can Read.	Census of 1880. Ten Years and Upwards. Cannot Read.	Percentage of Readers to Non-Readers.
Alabama	481,501	370,279	
Arkansas	378,647	153,229	
Florida	114,431	70,219	
Georgia	597,157	116,683	
Louisiana	351,758	297,312	
Mississippi	438,081	315,612	
North Carolina	592,061	367,890	63 37
South Carolina	345,676	321,780	
Tennessee	767,745	294,385	
Texas	807,973	256,223	
Virginia	698,539	360,495	
Total	5,573,569	3,254,107	

The proportion in the four Western States, already referred to, of readers to non-readers is 95¾ to 4¼.

The following shows those of ten years and upwards of the whites who cannot write:

STATES.	Census of 1880. Can Write.	Cannot Write.	Percentage of Writers to Non-Writers. Whites.
Alabama	340,955	111,767	
Arkansas	295,363	98,542	
Florida	79,374	19,763	
Georgia	435,013	128,934	
Louisiana	261,966	58,951	
Mississippi	271,818	53,148	
North Carolina	416,774	192,032	77⅗ 22⅖
South Carolina	212,931	59,774	
Tennessee	574,517	216,227	
Texas	685,015	123,912	
Virginia	515,892	114,692	
Total	4,092,678	1,107,042	

These two tables give a clear official view of the condition of general education in the South in 1880, and it is not believed that there has been any very great improvement since then, except in the cities.

We will now give two tables, showing the state of what may be called public intelligence and of the higher walks of cultivation. First in importance comes the press. The following table is from census of 1880:

STATES.	Dailies.	All Other Periodicals.	Circulation.	
			Dailies.	All Others.
South.	128	1,612	196,533	1,504,424
Other States	843	9,702	3,369,862	26,708,867

Rowell's Newspaper Directory for 1887 gives:

STATES.	Dailies.	Weeklies.	Monthlies
South	156	1,631	152
Other States.	1,155	9,485	1,503

Rowell gives no estimate of aggregate circulation, but he represents only one Southern paper having a daily circulation exceeding 15,000, only three exceeding 10,000, only four exceeding 7,500, only three exceeding 5,000, and only three exceeding 4,000.

As showing higher education, the following is taken from report of United States Commissioner of Education for 1884–'5: Number of university and college students in the South, 6,486; in other States, 27,891. This is a better showing as regards numbers, but we can judge better as to the quality of instruction, when we remember there is only one Southern university of national reputation—namely, the University of Virginia, while the other States have Yale, Harvard, Princeton, Cornell, Johns Hopkins, Stevens' Institute of Technology, and others that attract students from all parts of the United States.

As further showing the condition of higher cultivation in the South, it must be borne in mind that though we had and still have many men distinguished in law, medicine and politics, we have had and still have very few men noted in mechanics, science, art, literature, invention.

As bearing also on this point an examination of Johnson's Encyclopædia, an American work of standard authority, shows that only one editor, A. H. Stevens, out of thirty-one, was Southern, and only thirty out of 730 writers on special subjects were Southern, among whom were Beauregard, Lamar, Hampton, Curry. There were thousands of other contributors, of whom the South doubtless supplied some, but the names of these sub-writers are not given. It is not to be expected that a large proportion of contributors would be Southern, but the fact of so exceedingly few having been engaged may well prove a great dearth of higher education.

Having now given a very general and cursory, but not, it is believed, an unfair or inaccurate survey of the state of education in the South, let us now look at the subject more in detail, so that we may accurately perceive the conditions and the difficulties surrounding the question, because until we get this view we will not be in a situation to take the essential steps to disseminate education among *all* the people.

Chapter XVI.

— -

EDUCATION CONTINUED.

Private and Voluntary, or Public and Compulsory, Schools only
Methods of Combatting Ignorance—South Dependent on
Wretched Public Schools—Tables of School Population and
Number to Square Mile in Southern States and in Four
Western States—Number of Square Miles Required for Ave-
rage School of Thirty—Percentage of School Attendance—
Average Pay of School-Teachers and Average Day's Attend-
ance in South—With Separate Schools Education Impossible
and Prosperity a Delusion.

If education is not a prerequisite of progress and prosperity, or if among all the people sixty-three readers to
thirty-seven non-readers, or if among the whites alone
seventy-eight writers to twenty-two non-writers, is not a
bad condition of education, then this whole question of
education drops, and there is nothing more to be said;
but if education is a necessity of progress and prosperity,
if among all the people of ten years and upwards sixty-
three readers to thirty-seven non-readers, and among the
whites seventy-eight writers to twenty-two non-writers,
be a deplorable state of affairs, then a practical and press-
ing problem of the greatest and gravest magnitude con-
fronts us, and the question is, How shall we meet and solve
it? There are only two ways—namely, private and voluntary, or public and compulsory, schools. If all could
afford the expense of private schools, so that every neighborhood, however sparsely settled, could have a good

school, private schools would undoubtedly be the best
means of education, because they are flexible and can be
easily accommodated to local and personal conditions;
but the poverty of the South utterly precludes all possi-
bility of such a system, and therefore we are necessarily
thrown back upon public schools, with all their rigidity,
where children are stretched figuratively upon procrus-
tean beds and cut off or stretched out to accommodate
them to their inflexible system.   Public schools have now
taken the place of the Pharisee's Sunday, men being supposed to be made for Sunday and not Sunday for men,
and so children are now made for public schools and
not public schools for children.   But whatever their
faults, we are confined to public schools and must accommodate ourselves to them.

The conditions found in the South are poverty, sparse-
ness of population, great ignorance, and the forces to meet
and overcome these conditions are indifferent public
schools.   But such schools, which must necessarily continue indifferent, will never answer, and our only hope is
good public schools; and the question of how to get good
public schools is the one we have to solve.   In default
of money, there is only one way, and that is a large
clientage of pupils, for without many scholars there cannot be sufficient financial basis to secure good teachers,
and without good teachers good public schools are an
absolute impossibility.   Now let us see our basis for this
large clientage.   We will take the census of 1880 for our
guide, and we will include all children from seven to
nineteen years of age, which gives us a school period of
thirteen years.   We find by experience that an enrollment of fifty is requisite to secure average attendance

of thirty. We therefore calculate on the basis of enrollment of fifty.

STATES.	Children, 7 to 19. White.	Black.	Area Square Miles.	White, 7 to 19. Square Mile.	Black, 7 to 19. Square Mile.	School of 30. Square Mile. White.	Square Mile. Black.
Alabama	197,507	193,054	52,250	3.75	3.69	13.33	13.55
Arkansas	179,137	64,413	53,870	3.33	1.20	15.00	41.66
Florida	41,759	38,862	58,580	0.71	0.66	70.42	75.75
Georgia	240,596	232,955	59,475	4.06	4.05	12.31	12.31
Louisiana	135,503	141,932	48,720	2.80	2.90	17.14	17.24
Mississippi	144,078	209,041	46,810	3.08	4.45	16.23	11.00
North Carolina	252,510	171,604	52,250	4.83	3.28	10.35	15.24
South Carolina	112,447	189,968	30,570	3.67	6.21	13.62	8.05
Tennessee	354,841	131,025	42,050	8.41	3.12	5.93	16.00
Texas	349,393	129,725	265,780	1.31	0.49	38.16	102.00
Virginia	256,991	202,203	42,450	6.05	4.76	8.26	10.50

As a companion table, the following is given :

STATES.	Children, 7 to 19.	Area Square Miles.	Children, 7 to 19. Square Mile.	School of 50. No. Sq. Miles.
Illinois	920,304	56,650	16.25	3.08
Indiana	609,826	36,350	16.77	2.98
Michigan	452,597	58,915	7.68	6.51
Ohio	930,866	41,050	22.67	2.25

When we look at the first of these two tables we will
hardly be surprised at our illiteracy, when we see that
the two most thickly populated States, namely, Virginia
and Tennessee, required an area respectively of 8.26 and
5.93 square miles for a white school of thirty scholars,
and that Georgia, the Empire and model State, required
12.31 square miles, provided every white child and youth
between seven and nineteen actually attended school at
some period of the year.

But this difficulty of clientage is much increased, when
we take not the actual number of children—for very many
of these have not begun school by seven, and very many

more have left school before nineteen—but the enrollment
and average attendance.   Thus:

STATES.	Children, 7 to 19.	United States Bureau of Education. Report of 1884-'5.		Percentage of Attendance to Whole Population.
		Enroll- ment.	Average Attendance	
Alabama	390,561	233,909	144,572	11.45
Georgia.	473,551	291,505	195,035	12.65
North Carolina	424,114	298,166	185,578	13.26
Virginia	459,194	303,343	176,469	11.66

Applying the above percentage, which is actual experience, we find that only four years ago it required the following square miles respectively for white schools of thirty
scholars: 20.55, 17.44, 13.71, 12.40.   The number of thirty
scholars is selected, as already stated, for any less number
would not afford sufficient grading of pupils or compensation of teachers to make good schools.

Now, here is a physical impediment which can be overcome only by a large increase of population, and what
prospect is there of this increase?   Very little indeed, for
except in some of our few cities, and in several accessible
mining regions, where the increase is noteworthy, the
agricultural sections, which are the real South, are not
much more than holding their own in numbers.   In
order to have the school basis of Indiana and Illinois, the
States of Alabama and Georgia must more than quadru-
ple their white population, North Carolina must increase
hers three and a half times, and Virginia must increase
hers two and three-fourths fold.

The other Southern States, except Tennessee, are not
so favorably situated as the four already cited.

What is the prospect in this, or the next, or even in the
third generation, of this increase, or of anything like it?

And what, in the meantime, is to become of the education of the people?   The bulk of the white population will
necessarily remain uneducated, and many must continue

illiterate, and the States must inevitably fall behind in the race of prosperity and progress; and lacking in prosperity, they will as inevitably fall under the dominion of the other States of the Union.

Therefore, instead of increasing greatly in population, we may esteem ourselves fortunate if, in our ignorant condition, we be not deserted by the flower of our youth, attracted by prosperity elsewhere, and we thus be unable to hold our present numbers; and little or no increase of population taking place, there will be little if any improvement in our public schools.

According to the report of the United States Bureau of Education, the South spent in one year $8,475,993.00 for education, and we may continue for years to spend this vast sum annually, but it will be almost entirely thrown away in the country at large until we have a large enough white population to furnish children enough for schools, large and frequent enough and kept up long enough to attract an ample supply of competent teachers. Without good subaltern officers an army is little better than a mob, so without good teachers schools are little better than a mockery.

The following table shows the wretched implements our public school teachers must necessarily be, for they do not average the compensation of house-maids, who are likewise boarded, and shows how little schooling the children receive:

STATES.	Average Annual Pay of Teachers. Census of 1880.	Average School Days. United States Com. of Education, 1884–5.
Alabama.	$ 83 70	82.04
Arkansas	117 52	Not given.
Florida	86 16	95.
Georgia	100 25	Not given.
Louisiana	217 79	110.
Mississippi.	119 37	78.05
North Carolina.	52 46	62.
South Carolina.	96 20	70.
Tennessee	106 88	80.
Texas	105 54	100.
Virginia.	145 17	118.4

To fight the battle of education with our present forces and present system of separate schools seems well-nigh hopeless. But what shall we do? Shall we go on in our past and present wasteful and inefficient manner; shall we keep on and spend the little money we have and get small benefit from it, except in the cities and larger villages, or shall we look around for reinforcements in order to contend successfully with ignorance? If education is an essential of progress and prosperity, we must do it; and if we value education properly, we will search anxiously for these reinforcements; and if we only *will* it we shall gain our end, for the old adage is still true, "Where there is a will there is a way." But they are not to be procured by wishes or even by prayers, but only by action, and by action, too, that will clash with all of our preconceived ideas, that will be distasteful and repugnant to our prejudices, but not to reason and justice. But if we are serious in our desires for prosperity, we will not let them deter us, for to stumble and falter at things that are distasteful and repugnant is at once to put a stop to all progress, physical, moral and intellectual, for what in reality is progress but the overcoming of prejudice and hostility?

The rise and triumph of Christianity itself was simply an overcoming of the violent prejudices and repugnances of the civilized world; and, in truth, all reforms, and the more beneficial the reform the greater generally are the obstructions to be overcome, are contests against, and finally victories over, what is distasteful and repugnant. Volumes, and exceedingly interesting ones, too, could be written about reforms gained in spite of what was distasteful, and of reforms yet delayed, but still to come, because of distaste and repugnance, active and violent or phlegmatic, but deep-seated. To say, therefore, that our reinforcements are distasteful and repugnant is really to say nothing against them, and is no reason why we, if wise, should reject them. Our interest is to examine these reinforce-

ments and see if they will be efficient aids to escape from
our great and deplorable ignorance, and if found to be
feasible and practical, and especially if found to be essential, we should embrace and set them in motion without
delay.   Our impulse will be to say: impossible, or the
thing shall never be done; but we should be very chary
in saying anything is impossible, or that such a thing
shall never be, in view of what has taken place and in
view of what we have agreed to in the past quarter century.   In that time we have seen slaves made freedmen
at the scratch of one man's pen; by a simple " Be it
enacted" we have seen freedmen made citizens, legislators, jurors, teachers of youth, &c., &c.; we have seen
civil and political society completely changed, and social
life profoundly modified; in a word, we are living in a
new world, and we have assented to all these fundamental
changes that have made the new world.

Now, no changes in the future can ever be so radical as
those of the past, and therefore we should never again
say anything is impossible, or that we shall never permit
it until after we have given the subject a fair, deliberate
and impartial consideration.   And so, in the remedy proposed to educate our people, we should, in our own interest, hear calmly and fairly before striking.   If what is
proposed is impracticable, condemn it and let it perish;
but if it is necessary and feasible, even though very hard
and difficult, we may be sure that time will bring the end
about in spite of any opposition we may make; or that if
we persistently refuse, Southern society must continue to
lie not only in a bed of ignorance, but of poverty, too.

5

CHAPTER XVII.

EDUCATION CONTINUED.

Remedy Proposed—The Abandonment of Separate Schools—
The Necessity Thereof and Why—It Doubles Basis for Schools.
Separate Schools a Public Proclamation of Caste—Inferiority
of Negroes—Why They Render General Education Impossible—Their Tendency Radically Demoralizing—Differences
between Men Principally Differences of Education.

The remedy proposed is not a bread pill or some sooth-
ing syrup, but is a radical and far-reaching one, and is
no less than the abandonment of the principle of separate schools, which principle is an efficient and certain
mode of dooming to perpetual ignorance both whites and
blacks in thinly-settled sections.

This remedy will, of course, as already said, be extremely distasteful, and will be violently opposed unless
its necessity and its advantages can be demonstrated, for
until this is done the whites will never consent to co-educa-
tion, but will prefer to remain ignorant. We will, then,
endeavor to show both the necessity and the advantage.

The necessity for the abandonment of separate schools
is dual—physical and moral. The physical necessity is
this: With our sparse population separate schools cannot
supply a clientage numerous enough to secure good
teachers, upon whom the efficiency of the public schools
is absolutely dependent, but the abandonment of separate schools at once doubles the school population in the
South at large, and at once furnishes a basis upon which
good public schools can be built. Thus, South Carolina,

instead of 3.67 white children, has 9.88 of all children to the square mile; Georgia, instead of 4.06, has 8.11, and Virginia, instead of 6.05, has 10.81, &c., ample enough basis for good public schools.

The moral necessity is this: Separate schools are a public proclamation to all of African or mixed blood that they are an inferior caste, fundamentally inferior and totally unfit to mingle on terms of equality with the superior caste. That this is not a temporary and ephemeral but a fundamental, and caste inferiority, is proven by the fact that opposition does not cease when the temporary inferiority ceases, but still operates, however cultured and refined the negro may be. Hence it follows that separate schools brand the stigma of degradation upon one-half of the population, irrespective of character and culture, and crushes their hope and self-respect, without which they can never become useful and valuable citizens. Life is hard enough and progress is slow enough with all the tonic of self-respect and with all the stimulus of hope, but deprived thereof, the boldest and the bravest among the white cease effort and relapse into despondency, despair or recklessness; but when we make our implement of elevation, namely our public schools, simply a branding iron for stamping the letter "D," degraded, upon the foreheads of millions of black fellow-citizens, we deliberately tear up by the roots all our other efforts for their amelioration. We can improve the beauty, strength, speed and usefulness of animals by careful feeding, housing and training, but we can never make men of human beings simply by attending, however carefully, to their physical necessities—meat and drink of the best quality and in the greatest abundance leave them animals still. We can only make men of them by cultivating and stimulating their higher and nobler natures, their mental and moral parts, and this can never be done while the principle of separate schools remains in full force.

We can never stamp out illiteracy in the South at large as long as this principle is closely followed, for it requires that if there are not whites enough to form a separate school, then all such must remain ignorant, and if not enough blacks to form a separate school, then all the blacks must remain ignorant; and as these conditions are found everywhere in the South, general ignorance of course follows. In cities, large villages, and populous neighborhoods, separate schools may very well, as a matter of convenience, just as in the case of segregation of the sects where co-equality is acknowledged, be kept up, provided, however, that no children are on account of color excluded from convenient schools and forced to attend inconvenient schools; but if they are, then separate schools become an engine of degradation.

If we could arrange matters, we would be somewhat like the preacher of a New England fishing village in his prayers for favorable winds for the fishing smacks. If he prayed for fair winds for those going fishing, he necessarily prayed for bad wind for those returning from fishing. So what does he do? Not wishing of course to offend any of his flock, he beseeches the Almighty for a fresh but not violent *side* wind. So if we had the management of, or if prayers prevailed in the school realm, there should be just enough of each color in every neighborhood to form a good school, and the homes should be so situated that each color would find it most convenient to attend its own school, and then everything would be lovely, because, in colloquial phrase, "The goose would then honk high."

But, alas, we have not the management, and people will locate themselves where there are sure to be either too many or not enough of each color; and, under the guidance of separate schools, thousands and hundreds of thousands must remain without instruction, and what are we going to do about it? Old ideas and old ways, oblivious of the fact that the whites must through this system be very great, if not the greatest, sufferers, because they have most to lose, and looking only at the despised blacks, oppose every change, for they really care very little whether the blacks ever become better than field hands in the country or boot-blacks and menials in the city.

But good sense and justice not being blinded by prejudice or proscription, and being keenly alive to the fact that not only is knowledge the parent of virtue, but that ignorance is the mother of depravity; and knowing that it is the ignorant generally who become food for the brothels, jails and penitentiaries, who are the main supporters and upholders of saloons and bar-rooms, and who fill most of the drunkards' graves, and who are the depredators upon the labors of the industrious; but good sense and justice say, their parents pay taxes and their children are therefore entitled to instruction, and they say further that even if their parents do not pay taxes, it is a shame to humanity and an injury to society to let any of these little ones grow up ignorant and untrained; and after the manner of One who was the incarnation of justice and good sense, as well as of mercy, they say to all the little ones, white and black alike, come unto us, and those whom separate schools would make outcasts they take in their arms and carry to school, where they will be taught to know right from wrong and trained to practice what they learn.

Justice and good sense proclaim that education is sight to the blind, hearing to the deaf, feet to the lame, and strength to the weak; that it is the one pearl of great price, and that as the husbandman in Scripture sold all that he had in order to procure it, so every people, so we of the South, should sacrifice means, prejudices, antipathies—everything, if necessary, so that all our children may be educated; for if we should have lost all and gained education, we are then in position to regain more than we have lost; but if we should have saved all and

lose education, then, like the fool who had gained the
world and lost his soul, we, through ignorance and illiteracy, will finally lose all that we were fondly imagining
that we were saving.   The differences between man and
man are principally the difference of education.   Bismarck, an untutored savage, would be the bold and cruel
leader of some bloodthirsty horde; Bismarck educated is
the ruling spirit of Europe's greatest empire, and all the
nations of the old world hang breathless upon his slightest political utterance.

Certain things cannot coexist.   In classic times it was
Rome or Carthage, with Patrick Henry it was liberty or
death, and the late war it was slavery or freedom; and so
now justice and good sense proclaim that separate schools
and general education cannot coexist.   To say, when
other portions of the country have in a great measure
condemned separate schools, that we cannot rise to the
occasion when the prize is the redemption of our country
from the disgrace and curse of ignorance, is to belittle
and dishonor ourselves.

Chapter XVIII.

EDUCATION CONTINUED.

Fear of Demoralization—Mixed Schools do not Mean Demoraliza-
tion of Whites but Elevation of Blacks—Influence Descends.
The Higher Demoralizes the Lower, not the Lower the
Higher—Example of Nurses—Of Playmates—The Mammy—
Examples of Higher Demoralizing Lower.

But while thousands are sincerely desirous of doing
full justice to the negro, they yet cling to separate schools
because of a dread of demoralization, which they fancy
is inseparable from mixed schools. Because they sometimes see degraded white men mix with negroes they
imagine they have been demoralized by the association,
though the fact is they did not mingle with the blacks
until they had become demoralized, and they therefore
imagine that the simple mingling of the two colors in
the same school, however guarded and however well regu-
lated the public schools were, would also cause demoralization. In this they are thoroughly illogical, for besides
forgetting that reputable colored people will not mingle
with degraded whites, they also overlook the fact that
from earliest childhood they have been subjected to intimate negro association, and yet they have not been
degraded; and if they were not demoralized by the unre-
strained influences of negro nurses at the very time the
mind and the heart are most susceptible to influence
of every kind, why should they fear demoralization for
their children when under the well-guarded restraint of
well-managed public schools? They can have no well-

grounded apprehension, and such fears are chimerical.
Moreover, they should bear in mind that influence,
whether demoralizing or elevating, is like the rain—it
descends. The higher ranks of society elevate or demoralize the lower, but rarely do the virtues or the vices of
the lower affect the higher one way or the other; and in
the mingling of the two colors in the public schools the
result would necessarily be not the degradation of the
higher but the elevation of the lower. It is impossible to
conceive of well-bred children preferring, to any extent,
the bad habits and language of unkempt and untrained
little negroes. Instead of being attracted, they will be
repelled by every manifestation of bad ways, bad language, and bad thoughts, just as the virtues of Spartan
children were invigorated by witnessing the vices of
helots. Even in separate schools, both private and public, children do not form many intimate acquaintances,
and in mixed schools there is little likelihood of white
children forming any intimacies with black children. It
will not of course be as agreeable to attend mixed as separate schools, but when it is narrowed down to almost no
good schools for a great part of the South, or good mixed
schools, it would seem to be the height of folly to allow
feeling or sentiment to rob us of the inestimable blessings
of education. Purists such as these ought not to enter
rail cars if they saw negroes therein, or they should get
out as soon as they saw one enter, and should walk to
their destination or return home, and after they get home
they should remain there, lest they be demoralized by
even the sight of a black skin. People and their children, so susceptible to contamination, should not have
negro cooks or maids, negro butlers or coachmen, for if
education in well-regulated public schools will engender
demoralization, then servants which come into close daily
contact with master and mistress, with young Master John
and young Miss Mary, will surely bestrew their paths with
frightful white moral wrecks.

If mere association in well-regulated public schools, where bad children will be closely watched or expelled, will cause demoralization, what an opportunity the "mammy" had to put in her deadly work. Most of us above thirty years of age had our mammy, and generally she was the first to receive us from the doctor's hands, and was the first to proclaim, with heart bursting with pride, the arrival of the fine baby. Up to the age of ten we saw as much, perhaps more, of the mammy than of the mother, and we loved her quite as well. The mammy first taught us to lisp and to walk, played with us and told us wonderful stories, taught us who made us and who redeemed us, dried our tears and soothed our bursting hearts, and saved us many a well-deserved whipping; nursed us kindly and faithfully in sickness, and if death, in spite of all, snatched away a little cherub, she mingled her tears without reproof with those of the mother. The mother might grow weary and faint, but the faithful mammy seemed never to weary, but was always patiently and lovingly at her post, and when her summons came to go up higher we laid her tenderly to rest. In the hands of the negro mammy we were as clay to the potter, but did she demoralize us? Thousands who are scattered over the land, and in whose memory the mammy holds a tender and an honored place, have but one response, "No."

And when we became youths and played with negro boys, went fishing and hunting with them, gathered berries and nuts together, climbed the same trees, and threw down apples and cherries to the girls and little boys whose legs were too short to grasp the trees; and when we became older, young men and maidens, and had colored body-servants and colored maids, who were constantly at our elbow, and who knew all our love affairs, &c., became we then demoralized? No; and why? For the simple reason that we were higher, and the higher are rarely, if ever, demoralized by the lower. Influence descends; and if we mingle in the same schools the whites will not be demoralized, because they are the higher, the nobler, the richer, but the blacks through the influence of the whites will be elevated. The danger of contamination will not be from black but from bad white children, for the latter will have constant and easy access to all, while the former will be naturally confined to association with their own color. For centuries the Southern whites have been intimately associated with the blacks, and have we become demoralized? And if not we can have no well-grounded fears of contamination from well-regulated public schools.

When the writer hears the cry of demoralization, born as he has been and lived as he has in Southern society, and knowing intimately its dark as well as its bright side, he can only smile and recall the old fable of the lamb muddying the wolf's drinking water. The morals of the blacks are bad, and they are doubtless very glad to receive the impure advances of the whites, but as a rule they are not the tempters but the tempted; they are passive, and if they are not sought by the whites they will rarely seek the latter. History, fiction, the drama, every-day life, all abundantly illustrate the demoralizing effects of the higher upon the lower walks of society. Books furnish thousands of instances, as we read in David Copperfield and Adam Bede, of the higher male destroying the virtue of the humble female, and although we hear sometimes of grooms marrying their masters' daughters, we have to hunt a very long time to find one instance of the lower male seducing the higher female; and so it is in the South in the intercourse of the two colors. The virtue of the white female is secured by the ease with which the higher white debauches the lower black. Demoralization, indeed! If the prophet Nathan were now alive, and were to be as plain-spoken as he was in David's time, few Southern men would dare, in his presence, to cry demoralization, lest he should point his finger at him and say, Thou art the man.

Chapter XIX.

OTHER INJURIOUS CONSEQUENCES OF SEPARATE SCHOOLS AND
OTHER ADVANTAGES OF MIXED SCHOOLS.

Separate Schools Mean Oligarchy, Caste, and not Democracy—
Inculcate Inequality at Beginning of Instruction, Cultivate
Autocracy and Haughtiness in Whites and Abasement and
Servility in Blacks—Emancipation, Negro Suffrage, Negroes
on Juries, &c., &c., proved Chimeras ; so will Mixed Schools.
Mixed Schools will Disseminate Correct Ideas of Liberty.

If we, as a people, are to be democratic and not oli-
garchic; and if, as individuals, we are to be all equal and
not some superiors and some inferiors, it must be not
through means of separate schools, but through schools
whose doors freely open to all within the school district;
but if we are not to be democratic, if there are to be permanent classes or castes among us, some of whom enjoy
privileges denied to others—in other words, if we are to
change our whole theory of government, then separate
schools based on color or caste are the most effective means
we can employ.

For as already said, separate schools are a public proclamation to the blacks that they are *so* degraded that no
improvement of mind, morals, manners and appearance
will ever fit them for admission to white schools; that a
gulf as impassable as that between Dives and Lazarus
separates them from the whites; impossible of being
crossed by the blacks because the whites forbid, and
impossible of being crossed by the whites because caste,
the most cruel, the most odious, the most blind of all the

devices of man to secure selfish advantage, forbids. Separate schools poison at its very source the stream whence
spring the best and noblest fruits of education, because
at the very beginning of instruction the little ones are
taught two dogmas—first, that white children are and
shall *forever* be fundamentally superior to black children;
and second, that black children are and *forever* shall be
fundamentally inferior to white children. At the fountain of education the doctrine of caste, which elsewhere is
being successfully combatted, is enshrined in fresh vigor
and authority, and it seizes with its rigid, icy grasp the
impressible minds of the children, and taints them, and
the blind superiority thereby inculcated fosters sentiments
of false pride, disregard of the rights of others, and unfeel-
ing haughtiness to all, regardless of color, whom they
deem inferiors; and the inferiority thereby taught the
blacks cultivates feelings of abasement and of servile fear
of all whom they consider superior—sentiments totally
destructive of manliness, courage and self-respect, the
noblest jewels in the character of man.

Separate schools are necessarily injurious to both colors. To the black they are a deliberate affront, and their
tendency is to keep the whole negro population in a
degraded condition; and they likewise tend to deteriorate
the character of the whites, for they make of them oli-
garchs, priding themselves not on their merits, but on
their status, despising all below them and contemning
labor, because labor is performed by menials and inferiors.

But mixed schools, which, at first blush, we so much
dread, are not half so shocking or so bad as were negro
emancipation, negro voting, negro law-making, negroes
sitting on juries, negroes riding in rail and street cars,
our lordly selves standing the meanwhile, negroes sleep-
ing in the same berths on Pullman cars, &c., &c.; but
where is our dread of them? Dissipated by experience.

And what will become of our dream of mixed schools? That, too, will be proved equally chimerical. The rearing of our children will have been very defective, and their virtues will be very feeble and sickly, if they will be demoralized by the negro children; and if they should be, it would only prove that white parents had been extremely negligent in raising their offspring; but they will not be demoralized. On the other hand, however, their fine appearance, their good breeding, and their virtuous ways will be constant bright examples which the black children will be continually imitating, and instead of bad manners, bad morals, and bad language spreading among our children, good language, good morals and good manners will spread among the black children. Entirely separated as the two races now are during education, the black children, not having the high white model constantly before their eyes, generally consider it a small disgrace to be ragged and dirty, to be vulgar and profane, to lie and to steal; and only after they come in contact with their betters during school hours can we expect very material improvement; but when this is done we may confidently look for a vast improvement in their dress, speech, habits and ways.

Another and incalculable advantage of mixed schools will be that the whites will be taught the valuable lesson needed to be learned by every citizen of a free country, that the difference between man and man is not color, but character and conduct—worth makes the man; want of it, the fellow, saith the poet—and when this lesson is thoroughly learned, then will be disarmed that baleful pride that leads them to regard themselves as superior simply by virtue of a lighter skin, and which teaches them that it is needless to attempt excellence by the acquisition of virtue and knowledge; for why labor and strive to excel when they already excel without toilsome effort? When children are taught, as separate schools practically

do, that superiority consists in a white skin, they will
naturally be satisfied with that kind of superiority, and
they will not willingly undergo the tedious, painful and
patient ordeal requisite to prepare them for superiority
in science, art, literature—in all the vast range of attain-
ments which make us to differ from our savage and barbarous ancestors.

One reason, most likely, why the South has always
shown, and still shows, so little intellectual development,
apart from law and politics, is because the whites have
been possessed of the idea that the height of superiority
is a white skin, and that they have been content with
that kind of eminence. Mixed schools will, in time,
emancipate us from this fallacy; but until they do, or
are in a fair way of doing so, it will be vain to look for
much indigenous intellectual vitality in the South, and
most of what may develop will be compelled to seek, as
in the past, its encouragement in communities where
ideas of human equality have fair play, and where they
are not throttled by caste. There are many Southern
men of capacity and influence in the North and West,
either attracted or forced there because they had no field
or no intellectual liberty in their native land. It is not
that Southern intellect is any way inferior to intellect
anywhere else, only in the South its exercise and development are cribbed, cabined and confined by inexorable
caste.

Chapter XX.

THE COLOR LINE.

Dangers of this Line—Who Draws It, Whites or Blacks?—
Whites Opposed to every Right Gained by Blacks, and Refuse
them All Office—Blacks when in Control Confer Offices on
Whites—Why Blacks Vote for Republicans and Against
Democrats.

Lines of demarkation in the social body, if attended
with enmity, are always injurious, because then the efforts
of the people, instead of being directed to the general
good, are turned against each other.

The theological line, now happily almost extinct, has
in its day wrought incalculable evil, irretrievably injuring
some countries, which still seem to lag superfluous upon
the stage of nations, and has absolutely destroyed great
empires once happy, rich and prosperous, but now
deserted and desolate wildernesses.

The race and other lines have also in their day
wrought untold havoc, and in recent days and smaller
spheres the Know-Nothing line, the Knights of Labor
line, the Sectional line, and many other lines, have joined
forces in working injury, enormous in the aggregate, to
the welfare and happiness of men.

Another line, sharply dividing the social structure, has
of recent years become painfully prominent, and is now
grimly confronting us, and that line is—

THE COLOR LINE,

a line certain to be most pernicious to our prosperity, if it
cannot, like the religious line, be obliterated.

This line is at present deep, black and broad, and
almost as impassable as that separating Lazarus and Dives;
and if nothing can be done to remove it, then Ichabod,
like a royal cipher, must be stamped on most things
Southern, for this line, as long as its dark shadow menaces
us, means perpetual discord and strife for all, or worse
slavery for the blacks than they have ever yet known, in
either of which event our prosperity is severed at its roots.

This line, in few words, is the division of the whites and
the blacks of the South into two hostile camps, working
in opposite directions, and seeking opposite ends—the
whites damning the blacks and their allies, and the blacks
presenting a solid front of opposition against the whites.
That this state of affairs is not healthy or natural, is apparent to all, but the fact that it undeniably exists, proves
that there must be some deep-seated causes in operation
to produce such an effect, and it behooves us to inquire
diligently and candidly what these causes are; and if of
our making, to do our part for their removal, or if of others'
making, to seek to produce amendment in them.   But
truth, and not party, must be our object.

It is a common impression among the whites that this
color line is drawn solely by the blacks, and *apparently*
this is so, but before deciding, it will be well to examine
the facts and judge accordingly.

Naturally, there are many antagonisms in the problem.
Thus:

Former Masters,	Former Slaves,
White,	Black,
Beauty,	Ugliness,
Wealth,	Indigence,
Knowledge,	Ignorance,
Intelligence,	Stupidity,
Refinement,	Degradation,

and many others unnecessary to mention, and these of
themselves are sufficient to create broad and deep lines of
demarkation, which would require years of patient wisdom
for their eradication.

These are natural and mutual antagonisms for which we are not responsible, but there are other antagonisms which are strictly artificial, and are of our own making, and for which somebody is responsible.

Thus we (the Southern whites) opposed with all our might—

> Negro emancipation,
> Negro civil rights,
> Negro ballot,
> Negro office-holding,
> Negro jurymen,

—and the negroes obtained all these cardinal and essential rights in spite of our most determined and bitter opposition.

In Virginia, we enacted degrading legislation, aimed solely at the negroes, namely, the

> Whipping-post, and
> Chain-gang,

the repeal of which was against our wishes. We also required a poll-tax prerequisite to voting, and we repealed that law solely because it was found to keep more whites than blacks from the polls.

And we still maintain in North Carolina a county government law, expressly designed and administered so that negroes are totally deprived of the benefit of their county majorities. And we still maintain in South Carolina a system of electoral machinery, designed especially to deprive the negroes of their political voice, and so worked that the end is effectually accomplished.

We also proclaim, both by words and acts, that negroes shall not hold office of any kind, however small—our leading paper of Virginia, the Richmond *Dispatch*, expressing the idea by saying, that as long as a white man capable of holding an office can be found that no negro, however worthy and capable, shall be appointed—that is to say, of the seven or more millions of negroes, of seven millions of

citizens, that not one of them, whatever his merits, shall hold
the smallest office in the land of his nativity, in the home
of his birth. Unclean, unclean is the sentence, and
unclean shall they ever be, if we can prevent; our sole
terms to the negro being perpetual inferiority and degradation, and an acquiescence by the negroes in this
degraded status.

But we will not call this drawing the color line, for the
negroes are the ones who do this.

But, then, let us see how the negroes acted in the days
of their supremacy, and how they act now. Even in
reconstruction times, when everything favored negro
supremacy, the negroes by no means confined offices and
official favors to their own color, but generally entrusted
them to the whites. And at present, how do they act
where they have control? Speaking for Virginia, no one
questions that the negroes enjoy a free vote and a fair
count, and that they are the strength of the Republican
party. Now, for four years, beginning with 1878, the
Republican party had absolute control of the State, but
during that period, was not every office, from senator to
county judges, and even to clerks in the State capitol,
given to the whites, and did not they elect white congressmen where their majority was unquestioned, and did
they not also, as a rule, send white men to the Legislature from counties they controlled? And now that
Republican supremacy has disappeared in the State, how
do the negroes act in the so-called black counties? Do
they say to the whites, as the whites say to them, "No
whites need apply?" No; on the contrary, they give the
whites about every sheriff, every treasurer, every commissioner of the revenue, every county and every circuit
court clerk, and they content themselves with being jus-
tices of the peace, janitors, and such like. Whatever their
other defects, the negroes, as a rule, have sense enough to
select for office-holders the best whites they can find in

their own party, and in default of them, they select the best Democrats attainable.

But, we say, they cannot fill the offices because of incompetency, or, if capable, from inability to give requisite security. This is true in great measure, but still they could, as so many white politicians seek continually to do, wreck if they could not rule, and they might say, as we do with regard to their holding office, rather than that the whites shall hold the offices, we will let things go to the devil; but no, they do not draw the color line, but freely bestow the offices upon the whites. From this example of the action of the negroes in Virginia, we should dismiss as unmanly and unwarrantable fears that ruin and disaster follow in the train of the free, untrammeled suffrage of the blacks. If a free ballot and a fair count mean negro rule, then we have negro rule in all of Tidewater Virginia. Now, who draws the color line, whites or blacks? Each man shall answer for himself.

We frequently hear the expression, "Oh, that the color line could be broken, and that the negroes would divide their votes between the Democratic and Republican parties;" and when we say so, we fondly imagine that the negroes are the only sinners, and we never for a moment suspect that we may be the sole impediment to this much desired division. It is greatly to be wished that this color line could be broken, for as long as it remains intact it is a great injury to our welfare and a great menace to our peace and prosperity; and as long as it lasts, statesmanship is absolutely impossible, and we will be perpetually consulting expediency, availability, and everything else but right and reason.

Now, as long as we maintain our present attitude, let us see what is the prospect of dividing the negro vote; or why should they vote for the Democrats, and why should they not vote for the Republicans. In the first place, who gave them freedom, the ballot, civil rights,

&c.? The Republicans. Who opposed all these things? We, the whites, who stand for the Democrats. Who raised them from slaves, with their lives belonging to others, to full-fledged citizens of the greatest country on earth? The Republicans; and who opposed this elevation? We, the whites.

And secondly, who extends them a helping hand politically, who offers them encouragement politically, and who promises to perfect and render practicable all the rights and privileges they now theoretically enjoy? The Republicans. And who says to them, "You negroes are not only now a degraded and inferior race, but you are also incapable of material elevation; therefore, you must be content to occupy permanently and eternally an inferior and degraded condition—you must be satisfied to be our menial servants, to be our hewers of wood and our drawers of water—this is the best we will do for you?" We, the whites.

Now, with these facts before us, how can we expect the negroes to be anything but enemies to the Democrats and friends to the Republicans? We cannot; and change is impossible as long as waters seek the sea or the skies water the earth. And, pray, who is to blame for this ominous and dangerous state of affairs? We or the negroes?

Again: As we are kind to the negroes individually, and as we do them many a service, when we ask or expect them to vote with us we are greatly surprised, and accuse them of ingratitude if, as they generally do, they decline. But we forget that most of our kindness to the negroes proceeds from the standpoint of condescension, and of assumed caste superiority, and we expect it to be received with humility and from a feeling of acknowledged caste inferiority; and if not so received by the negroes, they are thought impudent and impertinent, and the fountain of our kindness soon dries up. So when we ask the negro to vote with us he says to himself, "Yes, Mr. A. is a mighty good man, and he has done me a heap of kindness, but Mr. A. belongs to white man's party, and he's always gwine with his party, which is always dead against nigger. No, can't vote with him; must stick to my friends." It is as natural for the negro to vote against us as it is for us to vote against carpet-baggers and South-haters.

Again: We think it very heinous for negroes to persecute negroes for voting with us. Why should we? See what we do when Southern Democrats turn Republicans. We do not, at least in Virginia, persecute them physically, but at the very rumor of one doing so, we look askance at him, and turn the cold shoulder to him; and when the rumor becomes confirmed, sociability ceases, friendship cools, and he unmistakably loses social caste.

Now, these changes take place towards people whose party does not threaten us with perpetual inferiority and degradation. We cannot brook any turning to the Republicans, and yet we think it monstrous when negroes ostracise their own color, and even visit them with pains and penalties for joining those whose watchword for the seven millions of negroes is eternal degradation and perpetual inferiority. Strange, passing strange!

To break this dark and ominous color line rests with us, but we can only obliterate it by treating the negroes with equality and impartiality, and by according them cheerfully all the rights that we ourselves enjoy; and, unless we do so, the day is not far remote when we shall find that the sceptre has departed from our hands never to return until a new and wiser generation shall have come upon the stage.

Oligarchy, caste, vassalage, are the regnant spirit in the greater portion of the South, and no country can prosper under their weight. To prosper, their galling chains must be sundered; and if ever they are broken, as they surely will be, mixed schools, by disseminating correct ideas of personal liberty and equality, will bear an honorable part. Until the negro sees and feels that he can of right enter the school attended by his white neighbor, the brand of degradation must eat into and consume his soul.

CHAPTER XXI.

THE DANGERS THREATENED BY THE PRESENT CONDITION OF
THE NEGRO—DANGERS FROM WITHIN.

Enmity and Bitterness of Blacks to Whites; Causes Thereof—
Whites Opposed every Right Gained by Negroes—Special
Legislation against Blacks—Whites Deliberately Increasing
these Feelings—How?--By Seeking to Educate the Blacks to
be Content with an Inferior Status—Should be Educated to
the Utmost or every Negro School should be Closed—Three
Alternatives—Give the Blacks an Inch and they will take an
Ell—No—Why Reconstruction Days Impossible—What has
Occurred in Virginia.

Although the South presents a quiet and peaceful
aspect, we have no assurance that this condition of the
undisputed supremacy of the whites, and the undisputed
inferiority and degradation of the blacks, will continue
indefinitely, because this very state of affairs which seems
so satisfactory to our short-sighted selfishness has produced, and is daily producing, in the hearts of six millions of fellow-citizens a vast mass of smouldering enmity
and bitterness, only awaiting a favorable opportunity to
display itself. We have raised up an enemy, silent and
sullen, at our very doors, who, though he will never conquer, stands ever ready to vex and harass, and to league
with those who, for any cause, seek to upturn the present
order of affairs.

Inferior as the negroes undeniably are, they have sense
enough to see that the whites, as a caste, are their constant
and inveterate foes, not that individually they are harsh

and cruel, but they know that this kindness springs mainly from the same benevolence that prompts consideration for their horses and cattle, for their cats and dogs. They know that the whites will not maltreat them, provided they throw up their hands and quietly submit to their arbitrary will, but they also know that if they do not, they go to the wall, irrespective of right or wrong. They remember that the whites fought a long and bloody war, not desisting until absolutely exhausted, or until they literally had reached the last ditch, to keep them in servitude; that they organized Ku-Klux to render their freedom nugatory; that they violently opposed the Federal amendment granting suffrage; that civil rights were conferred in spite of all their efforts, and that generally they have opposed everything tending to their elevation. They know, also, that when this opposition is quiescent, it is only dormant, not dead, and that it springs into full vigor at the slightest alarm, for did not the appointment by Governor Cameron, of Virginia, of a few negro school trustees, suffice to hurl from power at the first subsequent election the Republican party, which then controlled every branch of the State government?

They also know that this opposition of the whites is still in full vigor, depriving them of some of their most valuable rights; for is there not now in full operation in North Carolina what is known as the County Government Law, whereby, for the purpose of depriving the negroes of the management of local affairs in counties where they are in the majority, the people of *all* the counties are debarred the right of electing their most important county officers? And do they not also know that the whites of the Palmetto State, for the same purpose of depriving the negroes of their electoral franchise, have instituted complicated elective machinery, whereby a number of ballot-boxes, seven, it is thought, must be opened at each and every precinct, and if a ballot is put

in the wrong box it is lost, thus hindering and bewilder-
ing, and practically disfranchising thousands of voters?
Imagine seven ballot-boxes being necessary to secure a
fair election in South Carolina, when only one is needful
in Virginia, and everywhere else. They know, too, that
the whites jealously exclude them from all offices,
however small, unless it be to clean spittoons, and to do
other such menial and degrading work. Now, these and
many other things, among them the whipping-post,
chain-gang, and prepayment of poll-tax before voting, all
now happily repealed, convince the negroes that the
whites, as a caste, are hostile to everything tending to
their free, equal and independent citizenship; and so
believing, can we be surprised at their persistent and
even blind opposition to everything advocated by the
ruling caste, or that rancor and bitterness necessarily
smoulder in their bosoms?   If they listened to the whites,
it would be a most wonderful instance of unnaturalism.
Hence the whites, instead of having six millions of friends
and co-workers in prosperity, as they should have if they
showed only a willingness to elevate the negro, have that
number of secret foes in their midst.

     But here we are confronted by a singular fact.   Instead
of seeking to diminish and finally eradicate this enmity,
we are taking deliberate measures to increase it. Indeed!
How?   Simply by seeking to educate the negroes, but
not to educate them to the full measure of manhood and
citizenship, but to educate them to be still inferiors, to be
still subordinate to ourselves, and to be content to occupy
the lower stratum while we occupy the upper.   Education
is not only to fill the mind with knowledge, but to make
men and citizens in the highest sense of the word; but
our idea of the education of the negro is to load him
with knowledge, but to abridge the process of making
him the best attainable man and citizen, and to arrest his
mental growth at a point permanently inferior to our own,

and, after having done this, to expect the negro to be satisfied. Although this is an impossibility, because a flat contradiction, we do not see it, but we go on and furnish not only common and high schools, but also normal schools and colleges. We should stop at once all education of the negro, shut up his every public school, and forbid all private negro schools, unless we are prepared to carry his education to its highest attainable point, and are willing to accept all its consequences—for every increase of education only increases and intensifies his present discontent and enmity. How? Because the more uneducated we keep him the less he perceives his wretched and degraded lot; therefore, the less dissatisfied with it, and the less enmity to his superiors. But educate or elevate him ten per cent., what then? That elevation, slight as it is, enables him to see more clearly his degraded condition, and to feel more keenly his disadvantages, and to be still more indisposed to his superiors. We go twenty per cent.—sight, feeling, enmity, are all intensified. At fifty per cent., being willing that the negroes be that much superior, but that much inferior, we call a halt. But at this point we find ourselves in a double dilemma. The negroes are now in a position to see ten-fold their degraded lot, and to feel ten-fold their disadvantages, and when the command "Halt!" is heard they will be little disposed to respond "Yea!" and being now more enlightened, they will be stronger, and they will demand a further advance to sixty, seventy, and will not be content until the full hundred mark is reached. But the whites will then be at a disadvantage, for having gone fifty per cent., they can give no *reason* for not conceding the demand for seventy, and then for eighty, and then for the full hundred. We should stop at once and retrace our steps or go forward to the end, for three alternatives await our present course. The negroes, being partially elevated, looking behind and seeing the horrible pit

whence they have escaped, and looking forward and seeing the immense benefits to be gained and almost within
their reach, will never cease their efforts until they have
gained the whole one hundred per cent., and are as free
and as equal citizens as the proudest whites. This is one
alternative. Or the whites, opposing all further advance,
will strenuously resist, and becoming embittered by
opposition will not rest until they have succeeded in completely disarming the blacks and reducing them to a condition of absolute and complete subordination and degradation. This is another alternative. Or neither side being
strong enough to have its way, there must be continual
and alternate defeats and victories, advances and retreats—
a perpetual strife and discord—and factions must rend
the community, in which event the State must languish
and prosperity disappear, for prosperity dwells only where
concord reigns. This is the third alternative. The first
means peace, happiness, prosperity for all; the other two
mean strife, sorrow, adversity for all. This, however, is
the age of reason, and we may therefore look forward with
confidence to the day when the first alternative, after many
difficulties, delays, and dangers, shall wear the crown of
victory. We older ones will not see that day, but our
grandchildren will, for the light of coming day already
irradiates the eastern sky.

But what of this smouldering enmity? It may mean
that society may at times be upset, and it may mean dis-
turbances of greater or less violence, and it may mean
only sullen but silent discontent; but it does mean that
the negroes will always be on the alert to welcome divisions in the white ranks, and to coalesce with any faction,
whether they be worthy citizens rebelling against corrupt
ring rule and seeking the public welfare, or are merely
unscrupulous adventurers in search of their own selfish
ends, for they will naturally say change for us has no ter-
rors, for we cannot possibly be worsted, being at the bot-

tom already; on the contrary, change for us is welcome because it may bring advantage. The whites, therefore, instead of bending all their time, thoughts, and energies, towards promoting prosperity, will be engaged in watch· ing the negroes to prevent such coalitions, or, having been formed, in circumventing them. Instead of working, the whites will rather be constantly on guard, and living, as it were, in entrenched camps. But granting the whites long and undisputed lease of power, the danger is not removed; only delayed, but intensified. Long lease of power begets bosses; bosses beget abuses; abuses beget frauds of all kinds in order to perpetuate themselves, and frauds, becoming unbearable, finally beget factions, upheavals, or even revolutions; and when faction or rev· olution controls public affairs, there is no predicting to what length resentment and revenge may not go.

But most people will say, "Give the negroes an inch, and they will take an ell; unless we deprive them of their political rights, their numerical superiority in some States and coalition in other States with ambitious and unscru· pulous whites will give them complete control of the South, and we will soon see again reconstruction days, when, led by scalawags and carpet-baggers, they wrecked all they controlled." Such reasoning is, however, alto- gether illogical and chimerical, and is begotten of unmanly timidity. It requires like conditions to produce like effects, but neither the times, nor the negroes, nor even the whites, are anything like, and can never be like, they were for a few years after the war. Then, with the negroes just enfranchised and enthused with most extravagant expectations, nothing was improbable or even impossible; but when the conduct of the negroes and their allies is compared with that of the peasantry of France during the Revolution, as set forth by Taine, one is amazed at the little evil they wrought. During that awful period France was plundered and brought to the verge of starvation by

her own children; her best people were exiled, murdered
or guillotined, and her fair bosom was converted into a
frightful scene of arson, pillage and bloodshed; but the
negroes and their allies merely stole. Reconstruction days
are as much of the past as are the fearful times of Tibe-
rius, of the Inquisition, of Thomas Cromwell, of the Reign
of Terror, and are no more likely to return; and those
who seek to excite our fears by preaching their return are
either blind, timid, or corrupt, and are unworthy of our
confidence. The negroes have learned a great deal the
past twenty-five years; they have learned in some degree
that their own welfare is bound up in good government,
and they would therefore be willing to hearken to and
coöperate with us, and thus keep affairs in the hands of
the worthiest, did we but show slight regard to all their
rights and privileges; and the only sure way for us permanently to maintain control is to make them sharers
with us in the honors and the privileges of government.
Our present attitude will forever repel them and make
them deaf to our most persuasive solicitations; change
that attitude to one of justice and fair dealing, and enough
will come to us to banish forever the dread of so-called
negro rule.

Having seen what may occur, let us now recall what
has occurred. Several years ago there was a split in the
Democratic party of Virginia on the subject of the State
debt. The minority, though led by able men, chief of
whom was General William Mahone, found itself helpless; but as the leaders were ambitious as well as able,
they seceded and sought the assistance of the negroes,
who responded promptly to the invitation, not that they
knew or cared anything about the debt, but they knew
the Democratic party was their enemy, and they knew
that they could not be injured and might be benefited;
or that if they could not in the end shout victory, they
could at least sing revenge. In a short time the minor-

ity, with the aid of the negroes, gained complete mastery of the State. A clean sweep of every office was made. Judges, school superintendents, and even directors of eleemosynary institutions, were turned out or legislated out, and in a year or two the Democratic party, which had controlled the State from its birth, was as impotent as it is in the Green Mountain State. Virginia was now a satrapy, and Mahone was its satrap. He set up one and he pulled down another, like a Pharaoh; he absolutely controlled all Federal appointments within the State, and he might, with great truth, say, as did the Grand Monarque, "I am the State." Bitter factions rent the State, families were divided, father from son, and brother from brother, and a great gloom settled upon the whites. They felt as if they had passed beneath portals upon which were inscribed, "He who enters here let him bid adieu to hope," for hope had seemed to have deserted the land. But even these were not reconstruction days. Such times, however, are liable to occur at any time as long as we say to the negroes, as we do to our pointer dogs, "Down, down," followed with the lash, if obedience is not instant. To escape such dangers, there is only one way—respect all the negroes' rights as scrupulously as we do our own.

Chapter XXII.

THE DANGERS THREATENED FROM THE PRESENT CONDITION OF THE NEGRO—DANGERS FROM WITHOUT.

Dangers of Sectionalism Not Removed by Emancipation, but Direction Changed—Weakness of the South Sure to Continue and to Increase—Tables Showing This—Constitution Impotent to Protect—Partisan Majority in Congress can Absolutely Disfranchise Every Southern State.

Although sectional divisions on the line of slavery are gone, sectional divisions on the line of geography and interest are still in full vigor. There are yet New England, Middle State, Western, Northwestern, and Pacific sections, all more or less united in interest and blood, and there is yet the Southern section, which is diverse in interest and lineage from the other sections.

In matters of national legislation, therefore, there are likely to be two great sections, namely, the South on one hand, and the North and West on the other hand; and what one section *specially* favors, the other section will probably oppose; and as sectional legislation has always been a great, and, we may say, an inevitable evil, so we must expect it in the future, for whatever is or seems to be for the advantage of a section will be advocated by that section, though the whole army of wise men and saints should arise from the dead and pronounce it wrong. Change conditions, but not change location, and New England and Pennsylvania would be for free trade, and the South would be for protection. The lever to move the world that Archimedes sought, but never found, is interest, or seeming interest. Take away our seeming interest in heaven, and every church will be closed in twelve months and the pastors be roughing it in the world instead of basking in the smiles and feeding on the adulations of the "sisters."

Having, then, still to deal with sections and sectional interests, let us inquire what are the prospects of the South for increasing, or even holding, her own in this sectional race or strife. Taking only the present thirty-eight States and adding Delaware, Maryland, West Virginia, Kentucky and Missouri to the eleven Southern States, the population in 1880 was respectively 17,622,381 and 31,748,959, and the area is respectively 901,740 and 1,185,020 square miles. Present representation in congress is—senate, 32 and 44, and house, 121 and 204.

Now, granting an equal ratio of increase of population in the two great sections, the proportion of the representatives in 1890 will, on the basis of thirty per cent. increase in population, be 157 and 265, and in 1900, on the same basis, 203 and 344, or the majority against us now of 83 will be increased to 108 and 141.

But this is not all. Back of the States lie a number of Territories, and before long they will be taking their places in the halls of legislation. Let us see how they will naturally divide as for or against the South :

FOR THE SOUTH.		AGAINST THE SOUTH.	
New Mexico.	122,580	Utah.	84,970
Arizona.	113,000	Washington	69,180
Indian.	64,690	Dakota.	149,100
		Idaho.	84,800
		Montana.	146,080
		Wyoming.	97,890
Total	300,270	Total	632,020

In course of time, therefore, certainly within ten years, the South, as a section, will be still further weakened—that is, relatively, as one to two, for at the most she can only expect to gain six senators and 300,270 square miles, while the opposing section gains twelve senators and 632,020 square miles. If Dakota succeeds in being divided the gain will be six to fourteen. In the house our relative increase will not be any greater and most probably much less. As showing that the new States will likely be anti-Southern, we note that nine States have been added to the Union since the annexation of Texas, and all except West Virginia are bitter Republican States. These are the opposing forces the South will have to meet on questions of a sectional character; and what is she going to do if they should arise, as they are sure to do?

The South feels safe under the shelter of the constitution, and allowing that that sacred instrument will not again be wrested from its true intent and meaning, although our past experience should teach us to place little dependence upon constitutions, is she then safe from partial, hostile or even revolutionary measures? Granting she has not only a majority but the whole of the supreme court, and granting she has the president too, she is not safe if sectionalism becomes aroused, and her safety line is not reached until she controls Supreme Court, Senate and House. How is this? Because both the Senate and the House are absolute judges of the election and qualification of its own members. Let us see, and let us take for example the denial of suffrage to the blacks. The South makes no denial of the charge, but defends it on the plea of necessity. This plea may satisfy us, and it will, because it *appears* to be for our benefit; but suppose the other sections are not satisfied, and that they demand a free vote and a fair count in the South, as well as everywhere else; and suppose, further, that the

Republican party gains the house, as it already controls the senate, what may it do? We will take for example the State of Georgia, and suppose that after the house is organized contestants from some or all the districts *allege* intimidation, what may follow?

Looking at the returns and finding that less than thirty thousand voters elected in 1886, ten congressmen, or, indeed, without looking at them at all, the House may unseat every congressman, and who, Supreme Court, Senate, President, can prevent? And what can prevent them from doing the same to every Southern State, and it completely deprive them of representation, or let them be represented by Republican contestants? Nothing except the public sentiment of their own section. And all the senate has to do is to refuse every Southern senator, on the ground that the Legislature of his State was not elected by a fair vote. The South will then be in a bad dilemma, either unrepresented or misrepresented, and there will be no limit to the arbitrary or revengeful legislation that may be enacted, and never again will a Democratic president be elected by her vote. To be weak and right is miserable; to be weak and wrong is deplorable. In the first case, one's right will be a powerful defense against wrong; in the last case, one has no defense, and his misfortune will excite no sympathy, but on the contrary, the verdict will be, served him right.

If the South wishes to bring this evil upon herself, let her continue in her present course, and she will have her wish gratified by the year 1900. The whites may by that time see themselves disfranchised by rejection of their representatives, or they may see themselves misrepresented by contestants who are most likely to be incompetent and revengeful. But if the whites wish to retain control of affairs they cannot begin too soon, not only to permit, but to encourage, the blacks to use their franchise freely and fully. Some congressmen and legislators will undoubtedly be lost thereby, but better many of them be lost, and thus mitigate the just enmity of the negroes and disarm sectional majorities, only too eager for pretexts. Sectionalism is powerful and irresistible when founded on right, but when founded on error, time and discussion will rob it of its venom.

While we disfranchise we give sectionalism a powerful lever to root us up, but when we give a free vote to every citizen and a fair count we need not fear sectionalism or anything else, for our right will be a panoply to protect us from all assaults. No man, no party, no section, can afford to plant itself upon a fallacy, much less upon a wrong; and when the South takes her stand upon practical denial of suffrage to her negro citizens she commits a monumental wrong, which must be atoned for by many tribulations. The people, the world, we ourselves, though nursing and defending our own wrongs, are opponents and enemies of the wrongs of others, and on this principle we shall have not only the violent opposition of the other sections, but they will be upheld by the sympathies of the world. As a general observes with delight the blunders of his adversary, and gloats over his victory in advance, so we may imagine our political enemies rejoicing over our wrong movements, and gloating over the idea that, in a few years, by the natural increase of their section, they will again by our errors be placed not only again in control of the National Government, but also in absolute control of the South itself. We may then call upon the Supreme Court, but our enemies will laugh at us, and, like the prophets and the priests of Baal, they will tell us, call louder, you don't call loud enough; the court is asleep or on a vacation; for by the power of congress of deciding upon the qualifications of its members, they can keep out every one of our representatives, or admit only those whose sentiments suit them. They will not even be under the necessity of tampering with the Supreme Court,

as was done during Grant's administration, because it will
be impotent and despised. When the other sections simply demand that the South shall allow the same unrestricted vote and the same untampered count in the election of congressmen and of legislators that elect senators,
we cannot say in reply, Oh ! the bloody shirt, but we shall
be speechless.

The South would make a tremendous ado, and very
rightly, too, if a Northern oligarchy of half the population
was to claim and assume the right to vote for the whole
population in the election of national representatives, and
it would make a greater ado still if an oligarchy of manufacturers were to exercise this right; but there is no substantial difference between this and what the South does
in relation to negro suffrage. The other sections will see,
if they do not already, that they are right, and they will
not cease their efforts until the South yields voluntarily
or is forced, and then after the South yields through com-
pulsion, we cannot blame others if we are forced to take
back seats until we have gone through a long probation.
Better surrender now with the honors of the war, or rather
with the honors of right, than to wait for years and then
surrender at discretion. If there is any truth in experience these are the only two alternatives.

If the South intends to maintain her present posture of
caste and practical denial of negro suffrage, she must, in
addition to stopping at once all education of the negroes,
place a close and lofty cordon around her, not only to prevent all ingress, but also all egress—that is to say, we must
shut ourselves out from the world as completely as China
did for many centuries, and we must now, in these days
of light and civilization, imitate China in the days of
ignorance and barbarism. She must at once cease her
pleadings, humiliating from their despairing urgency, to
Northern people to come down and take possession of and

develop her resources, although manhood and a very moderate sense of pride should make her develop them herself; but she should repel all who voluntarily come, and she should also forbid her citizens passing her boundaries and seeing what the world is thinking, saying and doing. As oxygen in the economy of nature, so is light, thought, intelligence to Southern politico-social economy. As oxygen corrodes and finally devours the dying and the dead, as it is destruction to everything that does not keep step with progress towards perfection, and will thus, in time, perhaps, by its removal of wrecks, obstructions and decaying matters, produce perfection, so light, thought, intelligence, will as inevitably upset or overturn everything that cannot approve itself on the ground of right and reason. If, therefore, we let others come in, our system of caste and denial of suffrage is at once put to the test of right and reason; and if we let our citizens go out into the world, their ideas on the same subject are at once put on the defense by everything they see in the moving, stirring and progressive outside world; and if our defenses are weak, then, like flimsy barriers against a current, they must inevitably give way: those who come among us, being born with different ideas, and those of our sons who have gone abroad and imbibed the spirit of the world, both coöperating to tear down what we are now so fondly and blindly upholding.

What reason can we give for our present stand but the fear that something may occur that would be injurious to the present order of affairs? But this is no better reason, but is the very same that has been offered since man assembled into a rude community, by all abuses, by all tyrants, by all despots. All these oppose change solely on the ground that the pleasant order of affairs of which they are the principal beneficiaries may be altered to their disadvantage, and to maintain the *status quo*, they resort to stripes, imprisonments, dungeons, and scaffolds. As light, intelligence, reason spread, they, like oxygen in the physical world, corrode and finally consume all such fallacies and sophisms, and at last evolve from corruptions, abuses and tyrannies of all kinds, the beautiful and beneficent structure of liberty and equality, when all can say they are equal citizens of an equal government. But the South cannot stand this acid test of light, intelligence and reason, and, therefore, if she intends to maintain her present status, she must, in addition to all her other methods, exclude all from without and constrain all within to remain within.

CHAPTER XXIII.

WHAT OF THE FUTURE?

Present Status Likely to Pass Away—Day Breaks.

If there be truth in the aphorism, "That where truth and error are free to combat, truth is sure finally to prevail," then there can be no doubt as to the ultimate issue of the conflict between caste and equality: caste is the essence of the political and social Southern problem, denial of the ballot being merely an incident of caste. On this question we are not left alone to reasoning, but we have as well experience in the world at large, but better still, we have experience in the South itself.

As already said, the world, meaning thereby individuals, communities and nations—the world, which is no meaningless term, but, in these modern days of quick communication, is a vast engine for the expression and dissemination of social and political influence, although it may be obstinately wedded to its own particular evils and abuses—is strongly inclined to force virtue on others and compel them to correct their abuses. All the world's a stage, doubtless, but all the world is likewise, in respect of abuses, a number of beleaguered camps, into which others are perpetually pouring hot shot and exploding bombs, shattering defences and uprooting errors and abuses of every kind; and so, if the South determines to maintain her present *status*, so foreign to modern enlightenment, she must prepare to defend her ground against all comers, for she may be sure that when the world is attacking other people's errors and abuses, she, too, will find adversaries at every point of the compass. People feel that when they are attacking others' errors, faults, vices, they are somehow condoning their own shortcomings, and, as the world will have the same feeling when attacking the errors and abuses of the South, we may be sure that the world will come up to the assault with great alacrity. The South, then, should be very sure of its ground before inviting the onslaught, for mere heavy battalions have a tendency to attract the favor of Providence; but heavy battalions, supported by right, reason and intelligence, are absolutely sure to conquer. If these truths are "self-evident, that all men are created equal; that they are endowed by their Creator with certain inalienable rights; that among these rights are life, liberty and the pursuit of happiness," then we have no defense for that caste upon which Southern society is built, or for denying to many, or even to a few, rights which we claim for the whites alone. But, denying these truths to be self-evident, or even denying them to be truths at all, what defense can we offer?

Shall we say color? We shall then be forced to define what we mean by color—whether we mean only the pure Caucasian, or the Caucasian and Semitic, or the Caucasian, Semitic and Mongolian, or the Caucasian, Semitic, Mongolian and Red Indian. We will be compelled not only to draw the line somewhere, but we shall be compelled to give sound reasons for drawing the line at the division we select. And will it be possible to do this? And if a *majority* to-day decides against black, and to-morrow against yellow, why may not a majority decide on another day to discriminate against one branch of the Caucasian, and again, as did the Know-Nothings, against all Caucasians who lived beyond certain limits of a small portion of North America? We can't defend color for a moment unless we contend for segregating every small portion of the human family, and decide in favor of

reverting the civilized world to its original savage and
barbaric elements, for "color," if carried out, leads logically and inevitably to this.

But we may take this stand : The negroes are ignorant,
are lazy, are mendacious, are dishonest, are licentious,
and are therefore utterly unworthy of social and political
equality. Granted, and granted to the fullest extent;
but the more degraded, the world will say, the greater
obligation resting upon us to rescue them from their
blighted and brutalized condition. We cannot deport
them, because they are too many, and we cannot get rid
of them in any other way. They are with us to remain,
and they are citizens, and the world will make it its
business to see that they are not arbitrarily kept in their
present condition. We can no more defend our attitude
towards the negroes than could the Algerian corsairs
defend their attitude to the Christian world; than can
despots defend their attitude to their subjects, or than
can state churches and powerful nobility defend their
attitude to the people—all of which have passed or will
pass away, and so will pass away the attitude of the
whites to the blacks.

Caste will struggle hard, as it always does when its
privileges are endangered, to maintain the present *status;*
but all its efforts will be in vain, and it must fall before
the assaults of the world, founded, as these assaults are,
upon right, reason and material good. The battle will
be long and obstinate; but darkness, oppression and
injustice will, and must, go down before the assaults
directed against them from all points of the enlightened
world. Victory may and will be deferred and delayed,
but it is sure.

But, as already said, we have not to depend upon reasoning; we have experience for our guide. Virginia is
much ahead of her Southern sisters in acknowledging
the rights of the negroes; but this is not because Vir-

ginians are superior naturally to their brethren, but simply because Virginia is nearer to the world, and is therefore more affected by its enlightening influences than are the more remote States; and the more she comes in contact with the world, the more fully will all the rights of the negro be accorded, and the greater will be their elevation, and the greater will be her prosperity. And what comes to pass in Virginia, will also, under enlightening influences, come to pass later in the other States, till finally distinctions of race and caste will disappear; society will become tolerably homogeneous, and will not be torn by conflicting and contending interests, and only such social distinctions will survive as we see at present in private life, where we associate only with those whom inclination selects. When society becomes homogeneous then, and only then, shall we behold the full and complete prosperity of the South.

Chapter XXIV.

In Vain to Preach Right until Interest is Shown to be on the Side of Right—Example of England and India, and of the Manufacturing States and Rest of the Country.

While the elevation of the negro is primarily a Southern question, it is not wholly so. You, too, if not as vitally, are also vitally interested therein; and I now address you on the same momentous subject.

You will observe that I have appealed little, if at all, to right, justice, morals, or religion, but that the burden of the argument has been dollars and cents, and the exhortation to elevate has not been because this was great or noble, but simply because it would be profitable. And this key-note of appeal to the pocket, which many will consider as ignoble, was deliberately struck, not because Southerners are worse than others or less susceptible to arguments of the loftiest kind, but simply because all experience proves that human nature must be interested on its material side before its intellectual and moral instincts can be permanently stimulated. In order to move men to practice justice and right they must first be convinced that it will be profitable for them to do so. Occasionally the individual by a supreme effort will sacrifice a great deal in order to do right, but never does a community voluntarily do right at the expense of seeming interest.

For example : Grand as Great Britain is, leader of civilization as she has been, foe to slavery everywhere as she was and is, cynosure of all peoples who struggle for liberty or aspire to constitutional government, will she, the lighthouse of the world, loose her iron grasp from the millions of India whom she euphemistically calls by the same name as Englishmen themselves—namely, subjects—as long as she finds it profitable to rule them by the sword, sheathed it may be, but ever ready to leap from its scabbard and to slay right and left? Never! In such case the cry of right is as the infant's wail in the hurricane's blast. Although Great Britain has no more right to hold these millions in subjection than these millions have to hold Great Britain—and every intelligent Englishman will say, True—yet does not this same Englishman, does not the Imperial Government, does not even Gladstone himself, as fair and honest a statesman as ever lived, uphold and defend this slavery of innumerable millions? And why? Simply because it is to the material good of England to hold them in chains.

Great Britain and India are linked together not by ties of friendship, equality, and mutual interest, but rather by bands like the bridge built by Satan for the ruin of man from the gates of hell to the new-created earth. They are, as it were, bound together by a vast syphon, one end of which gathers up the riches of India and the other end discharges them in a broad, lavish and perennial stream into the pockets of Englishmen. In the face of such gain whistle to the winter's storm, rebuke ocean's billows mountains high dashing against the shore, call upon the dead slumbering in costly tombs or in graves unmarked by mound or slightest shrub, and you will be heeded sooner than by England when you speak of the rights of India, the sweat and blood of whose helpless children are coined into golden ducats for the benefit of her masters. In view of this benefit it seems to Englishmen no inconsistency to despoil the natives of almost everything except a girdle around the loins and a turban upon the head, and then spend a small portion of this enforced tribute in sending missionaries to convert them to the religion of their conquerors. No! They think they are thereby serving God acceptably. Mammon blinds the eye to every consideration of justice and equity, and we can get a hearing for these noble virtues only when we can show that our own welfare will be enhanced by observing them.

And so it is vain to preach to New England and Pennsylvania t! wrong—iniquity is not too strong a word—of wresting the legislative machinery of a common country to selfish ends as long as they find their riches increased enormously thereby. By this arbitrary and unjust legislative process they construct huge syphons, not one, as in the case of India and England, but many, all of which have their discharging ends resting upon their States, or rather upon their own particular employments, and their other ends, like monstrous measuring worms, stretch out menacingly and ominously towards the agricultural interests, and, settling upon them everywhere, drain them of their wealth. As long as this impoverishment of the one and this enrichment of the other can be maintained, what matters it to these States, and all similar beneficiaries, at what expense to others this profitable result is obtained. They care not if their legalized exactions bear onerously upon the vast majority, and are literally crushing to the six millions of Southern negroes, whose welfare the North claims to seek. Their poverty, great and grinding as it is, excites no commiseration in the breasts of these beneficiaries of partial and arbitrary laws, but on the contrary, through means of these laws they inexecrably demand tribute upon all the negroes wear, upon all tools and implements used in gaining their plain and scanty living, upon their medicines, their books, upon their very bibles—mind, body, and soul being laid under tribute—a small tribute, perhaps, upon the well-to-do and easy to be borne, but a crushing one to those whose means are more than represented by the widow's two mites.

What do these burdens, heavy and grievous to be borne, matter to those who reap the benefit of them? Nothing. On the contrary, no more satisfied than were the Romans with the spoil and plunder of conquered provinces, they demand more and still more. They exact taxes—partial taxes—not only for the support of government, but they demand, if taxes are not needed for government, taxes for the benefit of themselves—the public revenues to be absolutely thrown away rather than lift the burdens of others—and they literally demand that the world itself be shut out rather than allow any interference with their arbitrary privileges. Preach to such people of the injustice of such a course and you are talking to the deaf. No, not to the deaf, for they are conscious of some atmospheric vibrations, but to the dead, who will hear nothing less awakening than the blast of Gabriel's trump. Or, if allowing themselves to think for a moment of the galling poverty they are perpetuating, and if possible intensifying, among the millions of negroes, they quiet their consciences, as do the English in the case of India, by devoting an infinitessimal fragment of what they have wrung from these wretched creatures to sending them the gospel, and a few other thousands to educate them—mere drops in the sea, and as ineffectual.

The manufacturing States will never surrender their unrighteous hold upon the national legislature as long as they find it profitable, be the poverty of the agricultural States never so great; but the agricultural States themselves will support them until it can be proved to their satisfaction that so-called protection, in reality, decreasing their income and increasing their expenses, is greatly to their injury, and finally leads to their bankruptcy. Until their material interests are shown to be

injured, wrong, injustice, robbery, iniquity, as applied to
so-called protection, will be idle words. Therefore, in my
argument, ignoring every other motive, I have sought
only to show that the welfare of the whites themselves is
dependent upon the elevation of the negro, and until this
is done, to preach to the whites his elevation is as futile
as to preach to Englishmen " hands off India!" or to
New England and Pennsylvania "hands off congress!"
Until the ruling sentiment in each region is convinced
that equality is for its good, the negroes will be practical
slaves in the South, the people of India will be practical
slaves to England, and the people of the United States
will be practical slaves to New England and Pennsylvania.

Unenlightened human nature is the same everywhere—
following what seems to be for its interest; but, as self-
interest is generally blind, we are more apt to go astray
than go right, and therefore it is that it is necessary to
study patiently and industriously in order to see where
our true interest really lies. Apparent interest is usually
forward and obtrusive; real interest is frequently hidden
or obscure. The North worships the protection of manufactures; the South worships the protection of men—of a
caste. Both are wrong, for each advocates the protection
of a part at the expense of the whole.

CHAPTER XXV.

THE DUTY OF THE NORTH.

We must now discuss duties as well as material good—right as well as interest. We have hitherto confined ourselves almost solely to material good, and we have deliberately chosen what some may think a very low standpoint, not because Southerners are not responsive to rights and duties, or not because Northerners are *in esse* better than Southerners, but we have selected this point because all experience proves it vain to preach rights and duties when they are in conflict with what appears to be interest. But we can now discuss duties toward a large portion of our fellow-citizens, because your material interests are not so intimately involved.

You have duties to perform, and most serious ones, too, in the matter of the elevation of the negro, and the negroes have most valid claims upon you, and if you fail to perform them intelligently nature will demand a strict accounting at your hands. Although your interests are secondary to those of the South, they are yet great, because in a common country one great section cannot languish without the other sections, even the wealthy and prosperous manufacturing sections, suffering also, and *if* the prosperity of the South is dependent upon the elevation of the negro your prosperity is intimately associated with that of the South; hence, if you fail in your part, then you, too, cannot escape the penalty of the South remaining in a stagnant or declining condition in consequence of the negroes remaining in a state of degradation.

The *argumentum ad hominem*, in common parlance the argument that you do so yourself, although no argument at all, nevertheless performs the work of the most powerful and persuasive argument with the average of mankind. We see this every day. A man declines to be a Christian because some Christians are unfaithful to their profession. The manufacturer reduces his dozens to tens and his pounds to ounces, or adulterates his goods because other merchants do the same, and the Republican cheats at elections because he believes the Democrat does. If there is any or much self-denial required in doing right most of us decline to do so on the plea that so and so does wrong, and so the greatest impediment in the way of Southerners being willing to elevate the negro is because of your dereliction of duty towards him; because in the North the negro is frequently treated harshly and unjustly; because he is thrust in the back ground and is not given a fair chance.

Thus, although the negroes in some parts of the North enjoy many more privileges and exercise many more rights than in the South, especially in the far South, yet he still labors under many arbitrary and artificial disadvantages. Although in the great cities of New York, Boston and Philadelphia, and, most likely, elsewhere, negro children are admitted, as a matter of course, to white schools; and although the negro can travel anywhere without question, and can, with exceptions, attend churches, theatres, and official receptions, and put up at hotels, without fear of affront, yet, in the matter of employment, or of making a living, he labors under many drawbacks. Thus, while in the South, the negro may be laborer, mechanic, contractor, or what not, and is not molested by his white co-laborers, it is not so with you. Speaking as to New York city, the negro is not permitted to make his living except in the most degrading and servile spheres. He cannot work on the streets in public employment, not being allowed even to dig sewer trenches; he cannot work as painter, carpenter, mason, but he may tote bricks up a high ladder for the other men to do all the work; he cannot drive a truck, cab, or car; he cannot, except for his own color, be what his soul most delights in, namely, a barber; and there are many other things he cannot do without danger to his skull. In a word, he can do nothing that Patrick just arrived from the *Ould Counthry* chooses to consider an interference with his pleasures, profits, or even fancies. Evidently, Patrick thinks that if *he* is oppressed at home he ought to be allowed to oppress *somebody*, and finding, upon his arrival in our free and equal country, the weak negro, he, with the approval, tacit at least, of the North, of the party of great moral ideas, retaliates his wrongs upon him and drives him from all employment but the most menial and the least profitable. The pleasure of being cheated is stated to be as great as the pleasure of cheating, but Patrick evidently believes that the pleasure of oppressing the helpless negro is infinitely greater than the pleasure of being oppressed in Ireland. The only employments in which the negroes are allowed freely to engage are not those which develop independence and self-respect, and that bring ease and comfort, but those which breed servility, namely, waiters in hotels, gentlemen's coachmen and valets. Caste pursues and cripples the negro in the North as it does in the South.

It is probable that the negro meets with similar treatment generally in the North and West, because an employee of Kirk, a great soap manufacturer in Chicago, told me that on one occasion all Kirk's workmen, about eight hundred, struck because two negroes were employed in menial positions about the office, and the negroes had to go. This was chivalrous. Further: A lady who visited Columbus, Ohio, in September, 1888, remarked to me incidentally regarding the wretchedness, and even squalor,

7

of the many negroes she saw there and in other parts of Ohio, showing that the stronger and more intelligent whites had used the strength of a giant, not to uplift, but to keep the negroes in a condition of debasement. For negroes to earn in many parts of the North and West a comfortable and respectable living, they must work in the dark, selfishness seeming to begrudge them little beyond the fare of the prodigal son—the husks that even the swine refused to eat.

For the North to clear its skirts of the charge of hypocrisy, it must change its own treatment of the negro; for until it says, Follow my example instead of doing as I exhort, the seed it sows may be good, but it will fall upon hard and stony soil. Negroes being in development but children, the North, if it desires their elevation, must not be indifferent, or even unsympathizing; must not content itself with merely letting things drift, its conscience being satisfied if it places no obtructions in the way; but, as in the case of children, it must set itself resolutely and persistently to encourage them in every way. It is not enough to say be ye clothed and be ye fed, but it must take actual and practical steps to put them in the way of earning for themselves that food and that raiment. Instead of narrowing their range of employment, it should be expanded until commensurate with that of the whites. All employments and all offices should be open to them, and especially should all pains, penalties and persecutions inflicted upon them for the sin of color be punished with a firm and unsparing hand. You must create such a public sentiment that the community freely, cordially and practically recognize the fact as *fundamental*, as inalienable, that the negro enjoy as a right, and not as a privilege or condescension, all the advantages of civil society—such a public sentiment that the most reckless will no more dare to infringe the rights of the negro than of the white. But you must do more.

You must put yourself out of the way to encourage and to stimulate the hope and the self-respect of the negro, and you must lift from his shoulders the weight of the social structure which still crushes him into the dust. And, if necessary, in order to accomplish this great end, all your missionary societies, which are seeking to convert savages and barbarians in all the ends of the earth, should for a few years fix their eyes upon home, and devote all their men, all their means, and all their talents to convert the white heathen at their own doors—to convert themselves, practical heathen or infidels, as they are, respecting the rights of the blacks of their own households, and of the many millions in the South. To convert our own household, for whom we are responsible, would seem to be more acceptable service to our Maker than to go to the uttermost parts of the earth in search of those for whom we are slightly, if at all, responsible.

Put your own negroes in the way of supporting themselves with comfort, throw open all the avenues of life to them, encourage them to enter freely therein, relieve them of the danger and the dread of being robbed, beaten and imposed upon by their ruthless white neighbors; in short, elevate them to the full stature of citizenship, and then can you appeal with hope of success to your white Southern brethren; but until you do these things, your purest, most unselfish efforts will be looked upon with suspicion, and they will be frustrated by the fatal *argumentum ad hominem.*

FINIS.